Immigration to the United States

Jewish Immigrants

Richard Worth

Robert Asher, Ph.D., General Editor

Facts On File, Inc.

Immigration to the United States: Jewish Immigrants

Copyright © 2005 by Facts On File, Inc.

Facts On File, Inc.
132 West 31st Street
New York NY 10001

Library of Congress Cataloging-in-Publication Data
Worth, Richard.
    Jewish immigrants / Richard Worth ; Robert Asher, general editor.
        p. cm.
    Includes bibliographical references and index.
    ISBN 0-8160-5684-6
    1. Jews–United States–History. 2. Immigrants–United States–History. 3. Jews–United States–Social conditions. 4. Jews–Migrations. 5. United States–Emigration and immigration. 6. United States–Ethnic relations. I. Asher, Robert. II. Title.
    E184.35.W67 2004
    973'.04924–dc22
                                                                          2004017851

Facts On File books are available at special discounts when purchased in bulk quantities for businesses, associations, institutions, or sales promotions. Please call our Special Sales Department in New York at (212) 967-8800 or (800) 322-8755.

You can find Facts On File on the World Wide Web at http://www.factsonfile.com

Cover design by Cathy Rincon
A Creative Media Applications Production
Interior design: Fabia Wargin & Luís Leon
Editor: Laura Walsh
Copy editor: Laurie Lieb
Photo researcher: Jennifer Bright

Photo Credits:
p. 1 © The Granger Collection, New York; p. 4 © Hulton-Deutsch Collection/CORBIS; p. 11 © The Granger Collection, New York; p. 13 © The Granger Collection, New York; p. 17 © Bettmann/CORBIS; p. 20 © The Granger Collection, New York; p. 25 © NY Public Library; p. 28 © NY Public Library; p. 34 © Getty Images/Hulton Archive; p. 35 © CORBIS; p. 38 © Bettmann/CORBIS; p. 41 © Bettmann/CORBIS; p. 42 © CORBIS; p. 49 © CORBIS; p. 50 © Bettmann/CORBIS; p. 52 © Bettmann/CORBIS; p. 55 © Bettmann/CORBIS; p. 57 © Ellis Island Doc; p. 61 © Bettmann/CORBIS; p. 62 © John Springer Collection/CORBIS; p. 65 © AP Photo; p. 68 © Hulton-Deutsch Collection/CORBIS; p. 70 © Getty Images/Hulton Archive; p. 74 © David Rubinger/CORBIS; p. 79 © Roy Morsch/CORBIS; p. 82 © Richard T. Nowitz/CORBIS; p. 86 © AP Photo/Keystone, Yoshiko Kusano

Printed in the United States of America

VH PKG 10 9 8 7 6 5 4 3 2 1

This book is printed on acid-free paper.

Previous page: *Jewish immigrant boys gather in a tenement on New York City's Lower East Side for Talmud school, in which they learn about the writings of Judaism. In 1889, when this photograph was taken, the Lower East Side was home to most of the Jewish immigrants in the United States.*

Contents

A Nation
of Immigrants

Robert Asher, Ph.D.

Human beings have always moved from one place to another. Sometimes they have sought territory with more food or better economic conditions. Sometimes they have moved to escape poverty or been forced to flee from invaders who have taken over their territory. When people leave one country or region to settle in another, their movement is called emigration. When people come into a new country or region to settle, it is called immigration. The new arrivals are called immigrants.

People move from their home country to settle in a new land for two underlying reasons. The first reason is that negative conditions in their native land push them to leave. These are called "push factors." People are pushed to emigrate from their native land or region by such things as poverty, religious persecution, or political oppression.

The second reason that people emigrate is that positive conditions in the new country pull them to the new land. These are called "pull factors." People immigrate to new countries seeking opportunities that do not exist in their native country. Push and pull factors often work together. People leave poor conditions in one country seeking better conditions in another.

Sometimes people are forced to flee their homeland because of extreme hardship, war, or oppression. These immigrants to new lands are called refugees. During times of war or famine, large groups of refugees may immigrate to new countries in search of better conditions. Refugees have been on the move from the earliest recorded history. Even today, groups of refugees are forced to move from one country to another.

Pulled to America

For hundreds of years, people have been pulled to America seeking freedom and economic opportunity. America has always been a land of immigrants. The original settlers of America emigrated from Asia thousands of years ago. These first Americans were probably following animal herds in search of better hunting grounds. They migrated to America across a land bridge that connected the west coast of North America with Asia. As time passed, they spread throughout North and South America and established complex societies and cultures.

Beginning in the 1500s, a new group of immigrants came to America from Europe. The first European immigrants to America were volunteer sailors and soldiers who were promised rewards for their labor. Once settlements were established, small numbers of immigrants from Spain, Portugal, France, Holland, and England began to arrive. Some were rich, but most were poor. Most of these emigrants had to pay for the expensive ocean voyage from Europe to the Western Hemisphere by promising to work for four to seven years. They were called indentured servants. These emigrants were pushed out of Europe by religious persecution, high land prices, and poverty. They were pulled to America by reports of cheap, fertile land and by the promise of more religious freedom than they had in their homelands.

Many immigrants who arrived in America, however, did not come by choice. Convicts were forcibly transported from England to work in the American colonies. In addition, thousands of African men, women, and children were kidnapped in Africa and forced onto slave ships. They were transported to America and forced to work for European masters. While voluntary emigrants had some choice of which territory they would move to, involuntary immigrants had no choice at all. Slaves were forced to immigrate to America from the 1500s until about 1840. For voluntary immigrants, two things influenced where they settled once they arrived in the United States. First, immigrants usually settled where there were jobs. Second, they often settled in the same places as immigrants who had come before them, especially those who were relatives or who had come from the same village or town in their homeland. This is called chain migration. Immigrants felt more comfortable living among people whose language they understood and whom they might have known in the "old country."

Immigrants often came to America with particular skills that they had learned in their native countries. These included occupations such as carpentry, butchering, jewelry making, metal machining, and farming. Immigrants settled in places where they could find jobs using these skills.

In addition to skills, immigrant groups brought their languages, religions, and customs with them to the new land. Each of these many cultures has made unique contributions to American life. Each group has added to the multicultural society that is America today.

Waves of Immigration

Many immigrant groups came to America in waves. In the early 1800s, economic conditions in Europe were growing harsh. Famine in Ireland led to a massive push of emigration of Irish men and women to the United States. A similar number of

German farmers and urban workers migrated to America. They were attracted by high wages, a growing number of jobs, and low land prices. Starting in 1880, huge numbers of people in southern and eastern Europe, including Italians, Russians, Poles, and Greeks, were facing rising populations and poor economies. To escape these conditions, they chose to immigrate to the United States. In the first 10 years of the 20th century, immigration from Europe was in the millions each year, with a peak of 8 million immigrants in 1910. In the 1930s, thousands of Jewish immigrants fled religious persecution in Nazi Germany and came to America.

Becoming a Legal Immigrant

There were few limits on the number of immigrants that could come to America until 1924. That year, Congress limited immigration to the United States to only 100,000 per year. In 1965, the number of immigrants allowed into the United States each year was raised from 100,000 to 290,000. In 1986, Congress further relaxed immigration rules, especially for immigrants from Cuba and Haiti. The new law allowed 1.5 million legal immigrants to enter the United States in 1990. Since then, more than half a million people have legally immigrated to the United States each year.

Not everyone who wants to immigrate to the United States is allowed to do so. The number of people from other countries who may immigrate to America is determined by a federal law called the Immigration and Naturalization Act (INA). This law was first passed in 1952. It has been amended (changed) many times since then.

Following the terrorist attacks on the World Trade Center in New York City and the Pentagon in Washington, D.C., in 2001, Congress made significant changes in the INA. One important change was to make the agency that administers laws concerning immigrants and other people entering the United States part of the Department of Homeland Security (DHS). The DHS is responsible for protecting the United States from attacks by terrorists. The new immigration agency is called the Citizenship and Immigration Service (CIS). It replaced the previous agency, which was called the Immigration and Naturalization Service (INS).

When noncitizens enter the United States, they must obtain official permission from the government to stay in the country. This permission is called a visa. Visas are issued by the CIS for a specific time period. In order to remain in the country permanently, an immigrant must obtain a permanent resident visa, also called a green card. This document allows a person to live, work, and study in the United States for an unlimited amount of time.

To qualify for a green card, an immigrant must have a sponsor. In most cases, a sponsor is a member of the immigrant's family who is a U.S. citizen or holds a green card. The government sets an annual limit of 226,000 on the number of family members who may be sponsored for permanent residence. In addition, no more than 25,650 immigrants may come from any one country.

In addition to family members, there are two other main avenues to obtaining a green card. A person may be sponsored by a U.S. employer or may enter the Green Card Lottery. An employer may sponsor a person who has unique work qualifications. The Green Card Lottery randomly selects 50,000 winners each year to receive green cards. Applicants for the lottery may be from any country from which immigration is allowed by U.S. law.

However, a green card does not grant an immigrant U.S. citizenship. Many immigrants have chosen to become citizens of the United States. Legal immigrants who have lived in the United States for at least five years and who meet other requirements may apply to become naturalized citizens. Once these immigrants qualify for citizenship, they become full-fledged citizens and have all the rights, privileges, and obligations of other U.S. citizens.

Even with these newer laws, there are always more people who want to immigrate to the United States than are allowed by law. As a result, some people choose to come to the United States illegally. Illegal immigrants do not have permission from the U.S. government to enter the country. Since 1980, the number of illegal immigrants entering the United States, especially from Central and South America, has increased greatly. These illegal immigrants are pushed by poverty in their homelands and pulled by the hope of a better life in the United States. Illegal immigration cannot be exactly measured, but it is believed that between 1 million and 3 million illegal immigrants enter the United States each year.

This series, Immigration to the United States, describes the history of the immigrant groups that have come to the United States. Some came because of the pull of America and the hope of a better life. Others were pushed out of their homelands. Still others were forced to immigrate as slaves. Whatever the reasons for their arrival, each group has a unique story and has made a unique contribution to the American way of life. ❀

Right:
*A Jewish
immigrant
was
photographed
at his job at a
bakery on the
Lower East
Side of New
York City in
1910.*

Jewish Immigration

Seeking a Better Life

Throughout history, groups of immigrants have usually been identified by the countries from which they come. For example, Irish Americans come from Ireland, and Japanese Americans come from Japan. Jewish people, however, have immigrated to the United States from countries around the world. They are identified by their common religion, Judaism, rather than by nationality. Jewish immigrants began arriving in North America during the 17th century. They continue to immigrate to the United States today. The first Jewish immigrants came from Holland and England in western Europe. During the 19th century, hundreds of thousands of Jews immigrated to the United States from Germany and countries in eastern Europe. Others came from Asia, the Middle East, and South America.

Many Jews, no matter when they came to America, were pushed out of their homelands. They were fleeing anti-Semitism, or prejudice against Jews. In many European countries, Jews were not allowed to enter most professions, and they were often forced to live in sections of cities known as ghettos, away from other groups. Jews were also the victims of violent attacks called pogroms. When Jews came to America, they did not experience the type of persecution they had faced in Europe. Many Jewish immigrants became successful business leaders, entertainers, doctors, lawyers, and educators.

With the Jews came their religion—Judaism. This religion was different from the beliefs of Christians, who formed the majority of the American population. Jews observed different religious holidays, often ate different foods, and many Jews spoke an eastern European language known as Yiddish. Like other immigrants, Jews often formed their own communities in large U.S. cities.

Jewish immigration continued into and throughout the 20th century. In Europe, the Nazi dictator Adolf Hitler began a violent persecution of the Jews in Germany. Known as the Holocaust, it took the lives of an estimated 6 million Jews. After the war, many Jewish survivors of the Holocaust fled Europe for the United States. Others went to the new Jewish state of Israel. Gradually, Jews from Israel and other parts of the world began immigrating to the United States, pulled there by the economic opportunities available. By the 1950s, a combination of push and pull forces had given the United States the largest population of Jews in the world.

Although Jewish immigration has slowed during the 21st century, it is clear that Jewish Americans have made a huge impact on life in the United States. 🕎

Opposite: *New Amsterdam, the Dutch settlement that became New York City, is shown in this illustration. This is how New Amsterdam looked in 1656, two years after the first Jews came to live and work there.*

Chapter One

The First Jewish Immigrants

Living in Colonial America

Arriving in New Amsterdam

I n early September 1654, the Dutch ship *Saint Catherine* sailed into the harbor at New Amsterdam in view of the island of Manhattan. Several decades earlier, the Dutch West India Company had purchased the island from the local Indians. Then the Dutch had established a trading post at New Amsterdam (now known as New York City).

The governor of New Netherland, Peter Stuyvesant, was not pleased by the arrival of the *Saint Catherine*. Among the ship's passengers were 23 Jews from Holland. Stuyvesant referred to them as "repugnant," "deceitful," and "enemies . . . of Christ." Many people at that time were prejudiced against Jews because of the way they worshipped.

Most Jewish immigrants to the United States have come from these countries.

Israel

The word *Israel* means "the Jewish people" in Hebrew, their traditional language. The nation of Israel was established in 1948. Today, it includes most of the historical Jewish homeland in the Middle East called Palestine, which became home to the Jews about 2000 B.C. The northern part of this homeland was known as Israel.

According to tradition, Jews were descended from a tribe of people who had lived in Judah, an area of the Middle East, during Biblical times (about 4,000 years ago). Jews believe in a religion called Judaism. They also consider themselves members of a nation of people who share a common history. That history began in the ancient world when Jews in Egypt were persecuted for their religious beliefs. They worshipped one God, while the ancient Egyptians worshipped many gods. Eventually, a man named Moses led the Jews out of Egypt and gave his people the Ten Commandments, which were laws that the people were expected to obey. In the following centuries, the Jews ruled a kingdom in Palestine. Eventually, that kingdom was conquered, and the Jews lost their independence.

Many Jews migrated to Europe. However, they faced severe discrimination. For instance, Jews were not permitted to own land. They were often forced to live in small sections of European cities known as ghettos. In addition, Jews were driven out of many European countries or prevented from practicing their religion. In the late 15th century, for example, Spanish rulers King Ferdinand and Queen Isabella required that Jews convert to the Roman Catholic religion. Those Jews that did were called conversos. In 1492, Ferdinand and Isabella ordered all Jews who did not convert to leave Spain. For a short time, some of them went to Portugal. Five years later, however, the Portuguese king forced them out of his country as well.

Some of these Spanish and Portuguese Jews, known as Sephardim (or Sephardic Jews), moved to Holland. The Dutch (as the people in Holland are known) were far more tolerant of the Jews, many of whom were learned teachers and writers as well as successful merchants and craft workers. The Jews soon established a thriving community in the Dutch city of Amsterdam. Some Jews even invested in the new Dutch West India Company during the 17th century. By this time the Dutch had a huge trading empire in the islands of the Far East, the Caribbean, and in South America.

In the 1630s, some Dutch Jews left Amsterdam to live in the colony of Recife in the South American country of Brazil. The Jews of Recife built a synagogue, or Jewish house of worship. In 1641, a rabbi (a teacher and leader of the Jewish community) named Isaac Aboab da Fonseca came to Recife. He wrote the first Jewish hymn in the New World. In 1654, however, Recife was conquered by the Portuguese. Most Jews left Recife because they knew that the Portuguese would not allow them to practice their religion. Many returned to Amsterdam.

Twenty-three of these Jews, however, boarded the *Saint Catherine*. At first the ship tried to stop at the island of Jamaica in the Caribbean. But Jamaica was a Spanish colony, and the Jews were not welcome there. Eventually, the *Saint Catherine* reached New Amsterdam, where Governor Stuyvesant, too, tried to prevent the Jews from settling. In a letter to the Dutch West India Company, Stuyvesant said that with winter a few months away, these Jews might require the help of the colony to survive. This, the governor added, might be too much "for the benefit of this weak and newly-developing place." Therefore, he "deemed it useful to require them in a friendly way to depart."

However, the directors of the Dutch West India Company did not share the governor's prejudice. Some of the directors were Jews themselves. The directors also knew that the colony at New Amsterdam still had very few settlers and needed more. Therefore, it made no sense to turn away any new ones. The company's directors told Stuyvesant that the Jews could "travel and trade . . . and live and remain there, provided the poor among them shall not become a burden to the Company or to the community, but be supported by their own nation [other Jews]."

Governor Peter Stuyvesant of New Netherland was not happy with the presence of Jews in his colony. This portrait of Stuyvesant dates from the 1600s.

Early Jewish Settlements

The Dutch West India Company permitted the Jews of New Amsterdam to build houses in the new colony. However, the Jews were expected to live near each other and form a community, just as they had in both Holland and Brazil. Jews were also given some religious freedom. They could practice Judaism in their homes, but they were not allowed to build a synagogue in New Amsterdam.

A year after the arrival of the Jews at New Amsterdam, a few well-to-do Jewish merchants immigrated to the colony from Holland. They traded with American Indians at Fort

Orange (now called Albany, New York) on the Hudson River. The merchants also established a trading post in the Dutch colony to the south, along the Delaware River. But the Dutch colony in North America lasted only a short time. In 1660, New Amsterdam was conquered by the English, who renamed it New York.

The Kosher Diet

According to historian Arthur Hertzberg, the new settlers at New Amsterdam were "almost certainly the first Jews in America to observe the rituals of *kosher* cuisine." The term kosher refers to the Jewish tradition that Jews are permitted to eat only certain foods, as outlined in the Jewish dietary laws known as kashruth. The Jews believed that they had been ordered by God to observe this diet. For instance, Jews were not permitted to eat pork or shellfish. Other animals had to be killed by a method called *shehitah*. This meant that the animal had to be slaughtered as quickly and as painlessly as possible. Following a blessing, the animal was killed by a specially trained person, known as a *shohet*.

While the word *kosher* originally referred to the foods that Jews were permitted to eat, in the English language it has also come to signify anything that is permitted, legal, or honest.

Among the leading citizens of New York during the last part of the 17th century was a Sephardic Jew named Asser Levy. A successful trader in New York and Albany, Levy opened a kosher butcher shop in 1678. He was also permitted to own a house and serve as a member of a jury. Levy was the first Jew to be given these privileges in North America, most likely because he was a successful and respected business owner. At the time of his death in 1681, Levy was one of the wealthiest men in New York.

Another Sephardic Jew who was successful in business was Aaron Louzada. In 1700, he left New York and bought almost 900 acres (360 ha) in present-day Bound Brook in the English colony of New Jersey. The Louzadas continued to live in northern New Jersey throughout the colonial period.

In 1700, the Jewish population in North America was only about 250 people out of a total population of about 250,000. Even so, before 1706, Jews in New York City had created the first Jewish congregation, or religious community, in the American colonies. It was called Shearith Israel, or the Remnant of Israel. Unlike the Dutch, the English permitted the Jews to worship publicly.

Jewish Congregations in Colonial Cities

While the first Jewish congregation slowly grew in New York, others were being established in cities along the Atlantic seaboard. Among these was a congregation in Newport, Rhode Island. Since its founding earlier in the century, the Rhode Island colony had been very tolerant of religious differences, and Jews felt welcome there. During the 18th century, the Jewish population in Newport expanded. In addition to Sephardic Jews, Ashkenazi Jews had migrated to Newport. The Ashkenazim were German, Polish, and other eastern European Jews who spoke a language called Yiddish, different from the Spanish spoken by the Sephardic Jews. Like the Sephardim, the Ashkenazim had suffered severe persecution for their beliefs. As a result, they had left their homelands in eastern Europe for more tolerant countries, such as Holland and England. From those countries, they eventually emigrated to America.

*Touro Synagogue, in Newport, Rhode Island, was the first Jewish house
of worship in the United States. It opened its doors in 1763.
This illustration from the 1800s shows the synagogue as it looked
when it first opened.*

Jews believe in the idea of *Kelal Yisrael*. This means that Jews
have a responsibility to help other Jews. Therefore, when the
congregation in Newport was unable to afford to build a synagogue, it called on other congregations for help. One congregation that responded generously was Shearith Israel in New York.
With the help of Shearith Israel and of Jews in England and the
English colonies in the Caribbean, the first synagogue in
America opened in Newport in 1763. It was named Touro
Synagogue, after the congregation's rabbi, Isaac Touro. The
congregation called itself Yeshuat Israel, or Salvation of Israel.

Meanwhile, another Jewish community was being formed in
Charles Town, South Carolina. Jewish merchants and artisans
had immigrated to Charles Town during the late 17th century,

and Charles Town's Jewish community expanded during the 18th century. In 1762, a Jewish congregation opened the Coming Street Cemetery, the first Jewish cemetery in the South.

Another southern Jewish congregation was established in Savannah, Georgia. Among its leading members was Isaac Delyon. A merchant, Delyon traded rice and animal hides with business owners in Philadelphia, Pennsylvania. That city also had a small Jewish congregation, known as Kahal Kodesh Mikve Israel, or the Holy Congregation, the Hope of Israel. By the 1740s, it had established a Jewish cemetery and was holding religious ceremonies in the homes of its members.

Lives of the Jews

Most Jews in North America during the colonial period lived in cities—New York, Philadelphia, Newport, Charles Town, and Savannah—where they could work as merchants and artisans. Each of these cities was located in a colony that allowed its colonists to worship as they pleased. Even so, Jews throughout the colonies were not given the same rights as non-Jewish citizens. For instance, they could not hold public office. Other colonies were not at all tolerant. Boston, the major city in the Massachusetts colony, was an example. Few Jews went to Boston, which had been founded by a Christian religious sect called the Puritans. The Puritans did not encourage Jews to settle in Boston. Settlers there were required to pay a tax to support the Puritan churches, even if they did not attend those churches.

While most Jews lived in cities, a few migrated west. Jewish settlers owned land in areas such as western Pennsylvania, which in the 18th century was America's frontier. Jews who moved to the frontier apparently had a difficult time finding kosher meat or avoiding pork at their meals. As one observer, Peter Kalm, put it, "many of them (especially the young) when traveling did not make the least difficulty about eating this or any other meat." Haym Salomon, himself a Jew, commented that "there is very little [Jewishness] in Philadelphia," which had a substantial Jewish community. Indeed, some Jews seemed to have drifted away from their faith after coming to America.

In Philadelphia, David Salisbury Franks, a member of a prominent Jewish family, had gradually been assimilated into the Christian population. That is, he seemed to be far more a member of the Christian community than of the Jewish congregation. As a boy, Franks had attended the synagogue in New York, where he was born. According to historian Arthur Hertzburg, he also celebrated his bar mitzvah, the ritual that marks a Jewish boy's coming of age, when he reached 13. For this ritual occasion, Franks was required to learn selections from the Torah, the Jewish scroll that includes the first five books of the Bible, and recite them in front of the congregation at the synagogue. As an adult, however, Franks drifted away from his Jewish faith. He married a Gentile (non-Jewish) woman. Franks never became a member of the synagogue in Philadelphia.

It's a Fact!

Shabbat is the Hebrew word for "Sabbath." Jews light Shabbat candles in their homes just before sunset on Friday evening, when the Sabbath begins. Then they pray together at a service, followed by dinner. After the meal, they study the Torah. Families also attend services on Saturday. Shabbat ends at sunset Saturday evening.

Most colonial Jews, however, were active members of their congregations. Born in New York in 1696, Abigail Levy was one of them. She later married Jacob Franks, another member of the Franks family. Abigail Levy Franks regularly attended her synagogue on the Sabbath day. Called Shabbat, the Sabbath begins on Friday evening at sundown and lasts until Saturday evening. Abigail Franks ate kosher foods and wanted her children to marry only other Jews. However, since the Jewish population in the American colonies was so small, this was often very difficult. In 1743, one of Franks's daughters married a Gentile, Oliver DeLancy, a leading member of New York society.

Jews in the American Revolution

By 1770, the Jewish population in the colonies was about 2,500. That decade saw the beginning of the American Revolution. This conflict broke out between Great Britain and its North American colonies primarily over issues of taxation and representation in the British Parliament, or governing body. The colonists believed that Britain was taxing them unfairly since the colonists had no representatives to promote their interests in Parliament in London. Therefore, many colonists refused to pay a series of taxes imposed by Britain during the 1760s and 1770s. By 1775, this situation had led to war.

Most Jews supported the Patriot cause against the British. One Patriot was Haym Salomon, a Polish Jew and a well-to-do merchant in New York. When the British captured New York in 1776, Salomon, instead of cooperating with them, continued to support American independence by providing supplies to Patriot troops and convincing soldiers fighting for the British to desert (leave the army). The British arrested Salomon. He was about to be hanged when he escaped to Philadelphia. Eventually he worked with the French, who had declared their support of American independence. Later Salomon helped the Dutch government provide financial support to the American armies. Salomon also used his own money to help finance the new American government.

Another Jewish Patriot during the American Revolution was Mordecai Sheftall of Savannah, Georgia. During the war, he became commissary general of Georgia, in charge of providing food to the Continental soldiers. When the English attacked Savannah in 1778, Sheftall and his son were captured and put on board a British ship. To taunt him, the only meat the British gave Mordecai Sheftall to eat was pork, which he refused to take. Eventually the Sheftalls were shipped to the British colony of Antigua in the Caribbean. In 1780, Sheftall and his son were finally freed by the British and sailed to Philadelphia. The American Revolution ended the following year with the British surrender at Yorktown, Virginia.

The New Constitution

Although many Jews supported the struggle for American independence, they still did not enjoy the full rights of U.S. citizens. These restrictions began to change in 1787. That summer, representatives from each state met in Philadelphia to draft a new U.S. Constitution. According to Article 6 of the Constitution, "no religious test shall ever be required as a qualification to any office or public trust under the United States." This meant that Jews were no longer restricted from holding public office. In 1789, the Bill of Rights, the first ten amendments, or changes, to the Constitution, was approved. The First Amendment guaranteed freedom of religion. No longer could any state require Jews to provide financial support for other religions.

Opposite: *These Jewish peddlers were photographed on the Lower East Side of New York City, probably in the late 1800s.*

Chapter Two

A Nation of Peddlers

*Jewish Americans
in the Early 19th Century*

Achievement and Discrimination

In 1790, the Jewish congregations along the Atlantic coast sent a letter to the new president of the United States of America, George Washington. In the letter they called upon Washington to follow a policy that would allow "bigotry no sanction . . . persecution no assistance." In return, President Washington wrote, "In the enlightened age and in this land of equal liberty . . . a man's religious [beliefs] will not . . . deprive him the right of attaining and holding the highest Offices that are known to the United States."

Indeed, in the federal government, Jews were admitted to the "highest Offices," just as President Washington had said. David Salisbury Franks of Philadelphia became a distinguished diplomat. He represented the United States in France and later Morocco, in North Africa. Another Jew, Simon M. Levy, was admitted to the new military academy at West Point, New York. Levy graduated in 1802, the first Jew to achieve this honor.

However, although the U.S. Constitution guaranteed religious freedom and Washington had confirmed that the rights of Jews would be upheld, Jews still faced some discrimination. The so-called Sunday laws in each state, for example, prevented people from working on Sunday, the Christian Sabbath. However, they did work on the other six days. Since Jews celebrated their Sabbath day on Saturday, this meant that they were forced to stop work for two days. In addition, several states still prevented Jews from holding public office.

Even in the federal government, some Jews still faced discrimination. One of these was Mordecai Manuel Noah. Born in 1785, Noah left his home in Philadelphia in 1809 for Charleston, South

Carolina, where he became a newspaper editor. Noah wrote articles supporting the election of Democrat James Madison as president in 1812. After Madison's election, Noah was appointed a consul, or diplomat, in the North African nation of Tunis. As consul, Noah raised money to free Americans who had been taken prisoner by the pirates who operated along the North African coast. Noah's activities angered the Arab Tunisian government, especially because he was a Jew. Tunisian officials asked the U.S. government to replace him. Secretary of State James Monroe wrote to Noah, "At the time of your appointment as consul at Tunis, it was not known that the religion which you profess would form an obstacle to the exercise of your consular functions. Recent information, however . . . proves that it would produce a very unfavorable effect." Noah was fired from his job. Furious, he wrote a letter to the Department of State: "I thought I was a citizen of the United States, protected by the constitution in my religious, as well as in my civil, rights. . . . Admitting, then, that my religion had produced an unfavorable effect, no *official* notice should have been taken of it."

A New Wave of Immigrants

During the early days of the United States, the Jewish population remained small. But by the 1830s, a new wave of Jewish immigrants had begun moving to the United States. In 1820, only about 3,500 Jews lived in North America. By 1847, this number had grown to 50,000. The new immigrants came primarily from Germany, especially Bavaria, located in southern Germany.

Many of these Jewish immigrants were poor peddlers and shopkeepers. Some were craftsmen, or men who were skilled at a certain trade, such as butchers or tailors. They decided to leave Germany because the economy was getting more and more competitive, and work was becoming hard to find. They were also attracted by shipping companies that wanted to transport people to the United States. These companies published glowing accounts of the opportunities available in America. Jewish relatives who already lived in the United States encouraged the German Jews to move there.

Many Jews moved to New York City, where they made a living peddling second-hand clothing. On the southern end of Manhattan Island, one observer wrote that the "Jews were as thick, with their gloomy whiskers, as blackberries; the air smelt of old coats and hats, and the [alley ways] were glutted with dresses and over-coats." Other Jews established clothing businesses in Philadelphia and Baltimore, Maryland.

Peddling used clothing was a common profession for ambitious Jewish immigrants in New York City in the late 1800s.

However, some of the immigrants were not content to remain on the East Coast. They traveled westward to newer towns, including Cincinnati, Ohio; Chicago, Illinois; and St. Louis, located on the Mississippi River in Missouri. Leopold Mayer, a Jew living in Chicago in 1850, said that "relations between Jews and non-Jews were cordial." Jews, he said, were members of the volunteer fire department, and they attended dances given by Gentiles. They also had a variety of occupations. "Many were engaged in the cigar and tobacco business, and there was already a plumber . . . and even a carpenter here. Some—loading their goods upon a wagon, others upon their shoulders—followed the honorable vocation of peddling."

According to one estimate, there were approximately 10,000 peddlers in the United States by 1850, and the majority of them were Jews. With few stores in rural areas, peddlers provided the only chance for residents to shop. These Jewish peddlers carried clothing, brooms, buckets, pots and pans, and other items from the cities to remote farmhouses and small villages across America. Often they covered long distances carrying very heavy packs.

One of these peddlers, Abraham Kohn, had left Bavaria (a small country that became part of Germany) to live in the United States. Kohn had no choice but to make the best of his life as a peddler. One day when he was carrying his pack he saw another German peddler, named Samuel Zirndorfer. "Alas, how the poor devil looked," Kohn later wrote. "Thus one man with eighty pounds on his back meets another with fifty pounds on his back some four thousand miles away from their native town."

Levi Strauss

Levi Strauss was a Jewish immigrant from Bavaria who came to the United States with his two brothers. At first, they worked as peddlers in northern New York. But when gold was discovered in California in 1848, Strauss decided to travel by ship to San Francisco to try and make his fortune in the West.

Strauss brought some cloth with him, which he sold to the miners for clothing. He also used some canvas he had brought along to make pants for the men who worked in the gold mines.

Eventually, he sent a letter to his brothers telling them to "buy all the canvas . . . you can find."

Strauss had realized that the miners needed as many of the durable canvas pants as he could manufacture. Soon, he was joined by his brothers and together they started a clothing manufacturing company called Levi Strauss. The company later manufactured denim pants that became known simply as "Levis." Today the company continues to be a leading clothing manufacturer.

Some of these peddlers became successful enough to settle down and open stores in the small towns that were springing up across America. Jews established new communities in Denver (in the present-day state of Colorado) and San Francisco (in the present-day state of California). Others moved south to open businesses in Memphis, Tennessee; Natchez, Mississippi; and New Orleans, Louisiana. A few went to Texas, which until 1836 was part of Mexico.

Impact on Judaism

As Jews arrived in new communities, they often felt lonely. There were generally only a few other Jews in the area. These Jewish families banded together to form new congregations. Although these congregations were started to preserve the traditional Jewish faith, they also provided companionship for the Jews. Since these Jews had come from Germany, the new congregations carried on the Ashkenazic traditions. By the 1840s, they far outnumbered the Sephardic synagogues, which had been established earlier.

Meanwhile, changes also began to occur in the religious services in the synagogues. Many Jews started to leave behind the Orthodox, or traditional, rituals of European Judaism for new Reform services. In the Reform synagogues, men and women were permitted to sit together, instead of being separated as they were in Orthodox synagogues. Reform synagogues introduced organ music as part of the services. Prayers were read in English instead of Hebrew. (In Orthodox synagogues, prayers were printed in Hebrew, the language of ancient Jews.) Reform Jews also believed that the Talmud, the writings designed to serve as a guide to Jewish religious beliefs, had not been given to them directly by God, as Orthodox Jews believed.

Orthodox rabbis were strongly opposed to the changes of Reform Judaism, but other Jewish leaders embraced these changes. The leader of the Reform movement was Isaac Mayer Wise, who had arrived in the United States from Bohemia (part of the present-day Czech Republic in central Europe) in 1846. Instead of calling the house of worship a synagogue, Wise used the word *temple* to describe it. A choir sang in the temple, which used a book of prayers that Wise published in 1857. The book was called *Minhag America*, or "The American Rite." Wise spoke out repeatedly against discrimination against Jews in the United States.

Jewish Culture

As the number of Jews in the United States grew, they increased their contributions to American literature and education. Among the best-known Jewish writers in the 19th century was Rebekah Hyneman, whose poems appeared in a Jewish newspaper called *The Occident*. In 1853, she published a collection of her work, titled *The Leper and Other Poems*. One of her poems, *Israel's Trust*, begins:

> *Borne down beneath insulting foes,*
> *Defamed, dishonored, and oppressed . . .*
> *We are Thine own; we cling to thee*
> *As clings the tendril to the vine;*
> *Oh! Mid the world's bewildering maze,*
> *Still keep us Thine, forever Thine!*

Another Jew involved in education and literature was Rebecca Gratz of Philadelphia. Gratz regularly entertained famous writers at her home, including Washington Irving, author of "The Legend of Sleepy Hollow."

Gratz was very interested in Jewish education. In fact, many Jews knew that education was essential if they were to succeed as merchants, writers, and lawyers. The ability to read and write was of traditional importance to Jews, since throughout history they had lived in areas where others were hostile to them. An ability to read and write helped Jews preserve their culture while other groups worked to destroy it. This tradition of learning served the Jewish immigrants well in the United States.

In 1838, with financial support from Rebecca Gratz, the Hebrew Sunday School Society was started in Philadelphia. One child who attended the school recalled that all the children were taught in one large room with long windows:

> *Here Miss Gratz presided. A stately commanding figure, always neatly dressed in plain black, with thin white collar and cuffs, close-fitting bonnet over her curled front, which time never touched with grey, giving her, even in her most advanced years, a youthful appearance. Her eyes would pierce every part of the hall and often detect mischief which escaped the notice of the teachers.*

In addition to education, Gratz also devoted herself to charitable works. In 1819, she had helped found the Female Hebrew Benevolent Society of Philadelphia. In keeping with the spirit of *Kelal Yisrael,* or helping others, other Jewish charitable organizations were founded. One of the most important was the Independent Order of B'nai B'rith, founded in New York City in 1843 by 12 Jewish men. This organization, which was dedicated to helping the ill, the poor, widows, and orphans, attracted 700 members by the early 1850s. Branches of B'nai Brith also opened in other cities.

It's a Fact!

B'nai B'rith means "sons of the Covenant." The Covenant refers to the dedication of the Jewish people to serve God. B'nai B'rith was the first Jewish fraternal organization (similar to a club) in the world. Today B'nai B'rith is one of the world's leading volunteer organizations.

Jews and the Civil War

The coming of the American Civil War in 1861 split Jews, just as it led to disagreements among other groups of Americans, even within families. Jews who lived in the South generally supported the Confederate States of America. This was the new government made up of the southern states that had seceded from, or left, the Union. In the North, meanwhile, some Jews were abolitionists—that is, they were dedicated to ending slavery. Slavery, which was important to the economy of the South but hated by many in the North, was one of the issues that divided North from South and led to the Civil War.

During the Civil War, approximately 6,000 Jews enlisted in the armies of the North, while about 3,000 became Confederate soldiers. These were large numbers considering that there were only 150,000 Jews in the United States.

Dr. Jacob Da Silva Solis-Cohen, who served as a surgeon in the Union navy, wrote in a letter to the *Jewish Messenger* newspaper that most Jews in the army did not openly mention their religion. They feared that "it would expose them to the taunts and sneers of those among their comrades who have been in the habit of associating with the name of Jew everything that is mean and contemptible." Despite the discrimination and prejudice they faced, Jews proved themselves to be brave soldiers. Seven Jews were awarded the Congressional Medal of Honor, the highest award for bravery given to Union soldiers.

In the South, among the Confederate leaders was Judah Benjamin, a Jew. Benjamin was a lawyer in New Orleans and a successful plantation owner who had been elected a U.S. senator from Louisiana in 1852. During the Civil War, Benjamin served in the Confederate government as attorney general and later as secretary of war and as secretary of state.

Judah Benjamin, a New Orleans lawyer, was a Confederate leader during the Civil War.

The Confederate government, however, was unable to prevent the invasion of the South by northern armies. In 1862, Union forces led by General Ulysses Grant pushed southward into Tennessee. Grant believed that local southern merchants, especially Jews, were using unethical business practices to make money. In 1862 Grant issued General Order Number 11, which stated that all Jews who were living in the area had to leave. Some Jews may have indeed been guilty, but Jews were not the only ones involved in this activity. Furthermore, most Jews had no involvement at all in business. Nevertheless, approximately 2,500 Jews were given just twenty-four hours to leave their homes. Prominent Jews immediately contacted officials in Washington. They spoke to President Abraham Lincoln, who decided that Grant's order should not be carried out.

Nevertheless, General Order Number 11 showed that prejudice against Jews was a fact of life in America. During the Civil War, Jews were accused of profiteering—making huge profits by selling goods to the army. Jews were compared to the fictional character Shylock, a Jewish moneylender in William Shakespeare's play *The Merchant of Venice.* In the South, which was losing the war, Judah Benjamin was accused of betraying the Confederate cause. Benjamin was likened to Judas Iscariot, the man who had betrayed Jesus Christ. After the Confederacy surrendered in 1865, Benjamin fled the country.

Opposite: *A group of Jewish immigrants in New York City, photographed in 1908, hold bundles of matzo, or thin, flat bread typically eaten during the Jewish holiday of Passover.*

Chapter Three

New Waves of Immigration

From Poverty to Assimilation

Prosperity

I n the years after the Civil War, America enjoyed a period of economic prosperity. It was fueled in part by the growth of the railroads that crisscrossed their way from the eastern seaboard to the west coast. Major industries in the United States expanded, including steel, coal, meatpacking, and department stores. The American population also grew, enlarging towns and cities, while increasing consumer demand for new products.

Some Jews who had been in the United States for generations benefited from the boom times. Jewish bankers helped pay for the growth of railroads. In addition, companies such as Goldman, Sachs & Co., and Kuhn, Loeb & Co. became powerful investment firms on Wall Street. But Jews could not escape discrimination, no matter how wealthy they became. Exclusive private schools refused to admit their children. Directories of leading families in cities like New York and San Francisco did not include Jews. During the 1870s, wealthy banker Joseph Seligman was not permitted to enter the Grand Union Hotel, a plush resort in Saratoga Springs, New York. Well-to-do Jews retaliated by refusing to do business with the owner, Henry Hilton, costing him vast amounts of money.

Jews of Eastern Europe

T he discrimination experienced by American Jews was gener- ally mild, however, compared to the plight of the millions of Jews living in eastern Europe. Many of them were subjects of the Russian emperor, or czar, Alexander II. He forced most of these Jews to live in the so-called Pale of Settlement. This included areas of western Russian and a part of Poland that was controlled by the czar. Here the Jews lived in poor towns called shtetlach. During the 1870s, economic conditions inside the Russian empire grew worse for Jews. Few opportunities were available for most of the Jews of the shtetlach. In a shtetl, one Jew recalled,

you would see small houses, higgledy-piggledy, leaning all over each other. Some had straw roofs; if shingles, some broken. No cobbles on the streets. . . . Everywhere children, cats, geese, chickens, sometimes a goat, altogether making very strong smells and noises. Always the children were dirty and bare foot, always the dogs were skinny and mean, not Jewish dogs.

Residents of the shtetlach were constantly subjected to the harsh laws of the czar. The government forced young Jewish men to serve in the Russian army. Although families tried to keep their sons out of the service, the boys were often kidnapped by government agents and forced to serve. The Russian government also supported a policy of anti-Semitism. This encouraged other Russians to blame the Jews for the hard economic times that affected the country. In turn, Russians refused to do business with Jewish merchants. In 1881, Czar Alexander II was assassinated, and Jews were blamed for his death. Pogroms—brutal attacks on innocent Jews—broke out. Their homes and businesses were often destroyed. Meanwhile, more Jews were forced to leave their homes in other parts of Russia and move into the Pale of Settlement.

As a result of these conditions, Jews began a mass immigration to the United States. But these Jewish immigrants were not like the Jewish immigrants of earlier centuries. Although the earlier immigrants had also fled persecution, they were more likely to have some education, a bit of money in their pockets, or at least a trade or skill to offer. Most of the Jewish immigrants of the late 19th and early 20th centuries, however, had almost nothing. The terrible conditions in eastern Europe kept most of them uneducated and poor. But like the earlier immigrants, they had relatives and friends in the United States who had written about the "land of opportunity" that lay across the Atlantic Ocean. This acted as a powerful magnet pulling the Jews to the United States.

But immigration was not easy. Russian Jews had to make their way overland from Russia to Germany, board a boat to England, and take a steamship from there across the Atlantic Ocean to the United States. They needed passports, food to eat along the way, somewhere to stay while waiting for the ship to leave, and $34, a large amount of money in the 1880s, for the steamboat fare. (This is equal to about $630 in today's money.) Then the immigrants would have to endure a trip across the Atlantic Ocean of several weeks.

This illustration, made in 1885, shows Jews from St. Petersburg, Russia, waiting to board trains after being forced from their homes during the pogroms. The violence against Jews caused them to emigrate to the United States in huge numbers.

These immigrants could not afford comfortable shipboard rooms with a view of the ocean. Instead, they were crowded together below decks in steerage class. "We lay in the bottom of the boat," one immigrant recalled, "and rats jumped over us as we screamed. There was a big storm and the boat was crying like an old woman . . . and everybody was yelling that pretty soon the boat was going to break." Many immigrants suffered from seasickness. Others developed more serious diseases caused by rotten food or caught from other passengers.

Arriving in America

Most Jewish immigrants who came to America in the late 19th and early 20th centuries sailed into the bustling port of New York City. Most came through Ellis Island, the immigration station in New York Harbor, which opened in 1892. On one day in 1907, 11,747 immigrants from all over the world passed through Ellis Island.

Jews, like other immigrants, were given tags with numbers to identify them. They were lined up and directed to Ellis Island's Registry Room. Long lines often kept the immigrants in the Registry Room for many hours. Immigrants who could not speak English were examined by inspectors who spoke their language. The immigrants were asked their age, job skills, whether they were married or single, and where they were going to live. They were examined by doctors.

It's a Fact!

Emma Lazarus, a Jewish poet born in New York, wrote in 1883 about the arrival of the immigrants in her poem "The New Colossus." It contained the words, "Give me your tired, your poor, / Your huddled masses yearning to breathe free." These words were inscribed on the Statue of Liberty when it was erected in New York Harbor in 1886.

The sick were taken to the hospital on Ellis Island until they got well. Any immigrant who appeared too sick to be cured was denied entry to the United States and forced to return to Europe.

Conservative Judaism

During the late 19th century, as more Jewish immigrants arrived in America, Judaism began to change. A movement called Conservative Judaism arose during the 1880s. This brand of Judaism was a mixture of elements of both Orthodox and Reform Judaism. Some Conservative synagogues separated men from women (as was the practice in Orthodox congregations), while in others both sat together. Some allowed organ music, while others did not. In all congregations, men wore small skullcaps called yarmulkes. Overall, Conservative Jews permitted a flexible approach to the religious service as long as all members believed in the ancient traditions of the people of Israel.

Life for the Immigrants

About 75 percent of the Jewish immigrants who came to New York stayed to live in the city. At first, many Jews were overcome by the abundance they found in America, especially when it came to food, which had often been scarce in the shtetlach of Eastern Europe. One immigrant was struck by the variety of rolls he saw. "At first I could not eat enough . . . sweet rolls, plain rolls, with cinnamon and poppy seeds, without cinnamon and poppy seeds. . . . The soda fountains . . . gleamed majestically out of the open stalls and in the candy shops and spouted . . . carbonated water into a large glass at a price no higher than that of a bar of chocolate on the pushcarts."

These pushcarts crowded the streets of the Lower East Side of Manhattan, where many Jews lived. In addition to the pushcarts, from which vendors sold everything from candy to clothing, shops and outdoor stalls selling food and clothing lined Orchard and Hester Streets. Most Jews were fortunate to eke out a living from these jobs. They lived with their families in dark, dreary apartment buildings called tenements. Large families were crammed into one or two rooms, with little heat in winter and no windows to provide a breeze in the heat of summer.

At the beginning of the 20th century, when this photograph was taken, New York's Lower East Side was teeming with immigrant street vendors from all over the world, including Jews, selling all kinds of merchandise.

Author and photographer Jacob Riis described these immigrants in his book *How the Other Half Lives,* published in 1890. Riis takes the reader on a journey into a tenement building:

> *The hall is dark and you might stumble over the children pitching pennies back there. . . . The sinks are in the hallway, that all the tenants may have access—and all be poisoned alike by their summer stenches. Hear the pump squeak! It is the lullaby of tenement house babes. In summer, when a thousand thirsty throats pant for a cooling drink in this block, it is worked in vain. . . . That short hacking cough, that tiny helpless wail—what do they mean? . . . Oh! a sadly familiar story. . . . The child is dying with measles. With half a chance it might have lived; but it had none.*

Since their tenement apartments were often dark, stuffy, and unpleasant, immigrants on the Lower East Side usually spent much of their time outdoors, like these Jewish immigrants gathered on the steps and sidewalk, who were photographed around 1910.

Lilian Wald

Born into a successful Jewish family in Cincinnati, Ohio, in 1867, Lilian Wald trained as a nurse. She went to New York in 1893 and opened the Henry Street Settlement. The purpose of settlement houses, which were located in poor sections of cities such as New York and Chicago, was to help immigrants cope with their new lives. Settlement houses provided job training for young immigrants, libraries where they could find books to read, and nursing care. In 1915, Lilian Wald published *House on Henry Street*, a book describing her work in New York City.

Many immigrants made a meager living working in sweatshops on the Lower East Side. In the sweatshops, men, women, and children worked side by side making clothing. In a system called piecework, each worker was paid according to the number of pieces that he or she produced. The workers put in six-day weeks, from seven in the morning until eight o'clock in the evening, with only a half hour for lunch. Clara Lemlich, a labor leader, described the conditions in one of the sweatshops:

> *There is just one row of [sewing] machines that the daylight ever gets to—that is in the front row nearest the window. The girls at all the other rows of machines back in the shops have to work by gaslight, by day as well as by night. . . . The bosses in the shops are hardly what you would call educated men, and the girls to them are part of the machines they are running. They yell at the girls.*

In 1909, Lemlich, only 19 years old, led a strike of 20,000 shop workers. In order to persuade their bosses to improve their working conditions, the workers walked off the job. The strike, which was called "The Uprising," lasted 14 weeks. As a result of the strike, working hours were reduced to 52 per week (from about 78), and workers were also given four paid holidays.

The following year, another strike was organized by the International Ladies Garment Workers Union (ILGWU). Founded in 1900, the union included many Jewish workers. The successful strike enabled the ILGWU to achieve higher wages for its members. Despite these successes, however, most workers still toiled in unsafe conditions for unfair wages. Many factory owners continued to take advantage of their mostly immigrant workforces. It would take a tragedy to enforce any lasting change.

On March 25, 1911, a massive fire broke out at the Triangle Factory, a clothing manufacturer in New York City. One hundred forty-six workers, mainly young Jewish immigrant women, were killed in the blaze. When the fire broke out, the workers tried to escape, only to find that some of the factory's doors had been bolted shut. To escape the fire, some of the women jumped from the windows, dying as they hit the streets ten stories below. According to one newspaper report, "one policeman later related that he himself had seen 45 girls jump from the windows." The fire was already burning out of control by the time the fire department arrived on the scene. As firemen sprayed water on the building, some "who escaped the flames and smoke were later drowned by the huge streams of water." One eyewitness later said, "On sidewalks and the street were lying girls, dead, their clothes burned off them. Burning bodies were flying through the air. I was speechless from horror."

After the fire, workers, labor unions, and many others were determined that such a tragedy would never occur again. They worked with a renewed sense of purpose to make factories safer. Over the next five years, garment workers continued to stage strikes in order to force employers to guarantee them better wages and working conditions.

Speaking Yiddish

Every language borrows words from others. American English contains many words that were adopted from the languages of its immigrants. Here are a few Yiddish words:

kibitz: to interfere

mazel tov: congratulations

mensch: trustworthy or honorable person

mitzvah: act of kindness

nosh: to eat a bit

schlep: to drag around

shtick: routine used to get people's attention

The Jewish Press

The Triangle Factory fire was widely covered in New York newspapers, including the Yiddish press. There were five Yiddish daily papers in New York at the time. The Yiddish newspapers provided news coverage for Jewish immigrants. They also printed short stories and poetry. The most influential newspaper was *The Jewish Daily Forward,* which continues to be published today.

Perhaps its most famous editor was Abraham Cahan. Born in the eastern European country of Lithuania in 1860, Cahan lived on the Lower East Side of Manhattan and wrote articles and short stories. In 1897, he became editor of the *Forward.* The newspaper, under Cahan's direction, was aimed at the needs of working people. Its advice column, *Bintel Brief* (Yiddish for "a bundle of letters"), for example, helped Jewish immigrants adapt to the ways of American life. Jewish readers asked such questions as whether they should consider marrying Gentiles and how they should handle immigration problems.

Jewish Assimilation

Many of the issues confronting Jewish immigrants had to do with assimilation, or adapting to life in America. Some Jews adopted new American customs faster than others. Often a split occurred between generations of the Jewish immigrant population. Children, who attended the local schools and were taught in English, learned to embrace the American way of life. Jewish students also made friends with children from other ethnic groups. Many Jewish parents, however, preferred to preserve the old customs from Europe. They also tended to remain apart from other groups who lived in New York. Although they could technically live anywhere they wanted, poverty, discrimination, and a desire to stay near people similar to themselves kept these Jewish immigrants in crowded urban neighborhoods that began to resemble the ghettos they had been forced into in Europe.

During the early 20th century, assimilation became more difficult as Jews encountered more prejudice in American society. The large number of new immigrants, competing for jobs in New York and other cities, seemed to pose a threat to other workers. When economic downturns occurred, these workers blamed Jews for taking their jobs. Even well-to-do Jewish families who had been established in America for several generations felt the sting of this anti-Semitism.

Nevertheless, these successful Jews continued to help the poor immigrants by establishing new charitable organizations similar to B'nai B'rith and Rebecca Gratz's Female Hebrew Benevolent Society of Philadelphia. Through organizations such as the United Hebrew Charities, Jews donated many millions of dollars to build free medical facilities, shelters that provided food for the poor, and other services.

Poor Jews also helped themselves. They banded together in *landsmanshaften,* which were groups of immigrants who had come from the same areas of eastern Europe. Members of the *landsmanshaften* helped each other pay for medical care and funeral expenses. By grouping together this way, friends, family members, and others from the homeland could help each other in turn without feeling that they were accepting charity.

Succeeding in America

Frequently, the first generation of Jews who arrived from eastern Europe saw their main goal as creating a better life for their children. Many of them were successful at achieving this goal. An increasing number of young, second-generation Jewish Americans graduated from high school and began attending college, gaining far more education than their parents had ever achieved. Some even graduated from the Jewish Theological

It's a Fact!

One well-known playwright and short story writer was Sholem Rabinowitz, who changed his name to Sholem Aleichem (Yiddish for "peace be with you"). Born in Russia in 1859, Aleichem came to the United States in the early 20th century. One of his best-known characters, Tevya, was popularized in the play *Fiddler on the Roof,* which became a smash on Broadway in the 1960s.

Seminary in New York and became rabbis. Many young Jews became professionals—such as doctors, lawyers, and teachers—and moved away from the Lower East Side.

Some young Jews found a way out of the poor neighborhoods in the late 19th and early 20th centuries through the field of entertainment. Among them was movie star and singer Al Jolson, who grew up in Washington, D.C., and singer and comedian Fanny Brice, who grew up in New York City. As historian David Nasaw wrote, both entertainers "began their careers in similar fashion, singing or clowning on street corners and in backyards and alleyways with their friends. When they discovered that adults were willing to throw pennies their way, they quickly abandoned their amateur status."

Many Jewish entertainers performed in vaudeville. This popular, family-oriented type of theater included different performances, such as singers, comedians, and animal acts, on the same stage. According to one estimate, there were more than 2,000 vaudeville theaters in the United States and Canada by 1900.

Another form of entertainment was the Yiddish theater. During the 1880s, these theaters started opening in New York City. Among the best-known Yiddish playwrights was Boris Thomashefsky, who directed a company of actors that traveled around the United States presenting Yiddish plays. The company also presented Yiddish versions of plays by Gentile writers, such as William Shakespeare. In this way, the Yiddish theater helped Jewish immigrants break out of their eastern European traditions and exposed them to a broader culture. 🏵

Opposite: *Bolshevik soldiers marched through the streets of Moscow, Russia, in 1917. That year, in a takeover known as the Russian Revolution, they overthrew Czar Nicholas II, ending the czarist regime in Russia.*

Chapter Four

World War I

Changes in Europe

Anti-Semitism

B y 1913, New York had the largest Jewish population of any city in the world—1.6 million. However, Jewish immigrants to the United States still faced anti-Semitism. That year, the name Leo Frank was featured in newspaper headlines across the country. The Leo Frank case soon became identified with violent anti-Semitism in the United States.

Leo Frank was born in Cuero, Texas, in 1884, the son of German Jewish immigrants. When Leo was still a child, his family moved to Brooklyn, New York, where he grew up. Frank attended Cornell University and afterward moved to Atlanta, Georgia. Atlanta had the largest Jewish population in the South. In Atlanta, Frank became the manager of the National Pencil Company factory. He was also chosen to be president of the local chapter of B'nai B'rith.

Leo Frank, pictured here in 1915, was at the center of a trial that demonstrated the depth of anti-Semitism in the United States at the time.

In April 1913, the body of young Mary Phagan, an employee of the National Pencil Company, was found in the factory basement. Phagan's head had a bloody bruise, and she had been strangled. Her death had occurred on a day when the company was closed. At first, police investigating the case suspected Newt Lee, a night watchman at the plant. Lee was arrested. But investigators also believed that Leo Frank might be involved in the girl's death.

A friend of the victim told police that Frank had tried to begin a romantic relationship with Phagan. However, she had refused him. Police also found other women who said they had experienced similar advances from Frank. Finally, Frank was arrested. "My son is entirely innocent," his mother told the *Atlanta Constitution* newspaper, "but it is a terrible thing that even a shadow of suspicion should fall upon him."

The police also arrested James Conley, an African American who had recently been fired from his job as a sweeper at the pencil factory because of his long criminal record. According to Conley, Frank had paid him $200 to help move Phagan's body to the basement. Conley said that Frank had hit Phagan in the workroom near his office, killing her. Then he asked Conley for help in putting her body onto the elevator and transporting it to the basement.

At Frank's trial in August 1913, the jury listened carefully to testimony from Conley and other witnesses. The courtroom and the street outside were filled with people closely following the case. As one newspaper reporter wrote:

Mobs choked the area around the courthouse. Men with rifles stood at the open window, some aimed at the jury, some aimed at the judge. Over and over, louder and louder the men repeated the chant: 'Hang the Jew. Hang the Jew. . . . The mobs kept up their chant . . . spectators were allowed to give free vent to their anti-Semitism.

The jury took only about four hours to reach its verdict. They found Leo Frank guilty of the murder of Mary Phagan. The judge then sentenced

It's a Fact!

In 1913, as a result of the Leo Frank trial, B'nai B'rith established the Anti-Defamation League. Its role was to monitor and publicize incidents of anti-Semitism. The Anti-Defamation League of B'nai B'rith continues to play a vital role in combating prejudice against Jews.

Frank to be executed by hanging. Over the next two years, Frank's lawyers appealed the case to higher courts. There had never been any physical evidence—such as Phagan's blood on Frank's clothing—linking him to the murder. But on each appeal the guilty verdict was upheld. At the last moment, Georgia governor John Slaton decided that instead of being executed, Frank should remain in prison for life.

The Ku Klux Klan and Anti-Semitism

The Ku Klux Klan (also known as the KKK or the Klan) was founded in the South after the Civil War. Its members wore white hooded robes. Its goal was to prevent former African-American slaves from achieving power in the South. Among other things, the Klan murdered African Americans and found ways to prevent them from voting. By the end of the 19th century, membership in the Klan declined because discriminatory laws passed in southern states prevented African Americans from enjoying the same rights as white citizens. There was no longer any need for the Klan to do so. After the Leo Frank case, however, the Ku Klux Klan was revived in Georgia. (Klan members opposed equal rights not only for African Americans but also for immigrants and Jews.) By 1925, membership in the Klan was about 4 million. Klan members, dressed in their hooded robes, staged huge rallies in major cities, including Washington, D.C. In some states, Klan members refused to shop at stores owned by Jews. Klan newspapers accused Jews of conspiring to control the world. Klan members also burned wooden crosses in front of Jewish homes. Klan membership declined again during the late 1920s, after one of its members was convicted of murder. A further decline occurred during the Great Depression, during the 1930s. Members were required to pay dues, and few people could afford them at that time.

Governor Slaton had not been convinced by the evidence that Frank was guilty. He had also received letters from leading

Jews and other influential people asking him to prevent Frank's execution. "Two thousand years ago," Slaton said,

> *another Governor [Pontius Pilate, the Roman governor of Judea] washed his hands of a case and turned over a Jew [Jesus Christ] to a mob. For two thousand years that Governor's name has been accursed. If today another Jew were lying in his grave because I had failed to do my duty, I would all through life find his blood on my hands and would consider myself an assassin through cowardice.*

Many people in Georgia, however, did not support Governor Slaton's decision. There was even some talk of forming a mob, removing Frank from prison, where he was being held, and killing him. Inside the prison, Frank was attacked by another inmate who cut his throat. Shortly afterward, a group of 25 men armed with guns broke into the prison, dragged Frank away, and hanged him.

Pallbearers lift the coffin of Leo Frank in Marietta, Georgia, in August 1915. Frank was lynched by an anti-Semitic mob.

The men left Frank's body swaying from the tree, and sightseers later took pictures of it. Leo Frank's killing sent a message to many Jewish immigrants that they were not welcome in the United States.

American Jews and World War I

While Leo Frank's fate was being decided in the United States, a much larger crisis was occurring in Europe. In August 1914, World War I broke out. The war pitted the Allies (England, France, and Russia) against Germany and Austria-Hungary. Jews in America found themselves in an unusual position during the war. The United States had close ties to the Allies. But many Jews supported Germany, because their families were German immigrants. In addition, Jews from eastern Europe hated Russia's ruler, Czar Nicholas II. They had suffered during the Russian pogroms that were encouraged by the czarist government. For that reason, they were hesitant to support the Allies since Russia was one of them.

American Jewish Joint Distribution Committee

The American Jewish Joint Distribution Committee, known as the "Joint," was founded in New York in November 1914. Its purpose was to raise money among Jews in the United States to help Jewish refugees in war-torn Europe. The Joint, according to historian Howard Sachar, "would come to rank second only to the Red Cross as possibly the most efficient overseas relief [agency] in the world."

During the war, Jewish immigration declined. With battles raging across western Europe, few immigrants could leave for the United States. In 1917, U.S. president Woodrow Wilson declared war on Germany and joined the Allies. During the war, Jewish banker Bernard Baruch served as a close adviser to President Wilson. Baruch was in charge of supervising the effort by American industries to manufacture armaments for the war effort.

To provide soldiers for the war, the U.S. government began to draft, or require, men to serve in the armed forces. The draft created a problem for some Jews. It reminded eastern European Jews of efforts by the czar to force them into the Russian army. Therefore, some Jewish immigrants opposed the draft. However, 250,000 Jews did serve in the U.S. Army and U.S. Navy during the war. In fact, four Jews were awarded the Congressional Medal of Honor, America's highest honor for bravery in combat.

Louis D. Brandeis

In 1916, President Woodrow Wilson nominated Louis D. Brandeis to serve on the U.S. Supreme Court, the first Jew to be appointed to the Court. Because he was a Jew, Brandeis's nomination was very controversial. He was opposed by many members of the U.S. Senate, which had to approve his nomination.

Born in Louisville, Kentucky, in 1856, Brandeis later attended Harvard Law School. As an attorney, he took many cases defending the rights of small business owners against major corporations. In addition, Brandeis assisted labor unions in their efforts to achieve better working conditions. Brandeis served on the Supreme Court for 23 years and later became an adviser to President Franklin D. Roosevelt.

In 1917, during the fighting in Europe, the czarist government in Russia was overthrown. Jewish immigrants in the United States hailed the end of the czarist regime. As Abraham Cahan, editor of the *Forward,* put it, "It means freedom." Crowds of Jewish immigrants gathered on New York's Lower East Side to celebrate the end of czarist oppression. However, the new government of Russia lasted for only a year. Then it, too, was overthrown and replaced by a Communist dictatorship. In the Ukraine, located in western Russia, Jews became the victims of new pogroms. To help Jews in the Ukraine, Jews in the United States raised millions of dollars in financial aid.

In November 1918, the Allies finally achieved victory in World War I. The end of the war would create many changes for Jewish immigrants who wanted to leave Europe and live in the United States.

Opposite: *These identification papers were presented to U.S. immigration officials at Ellis Island by a Jewish immigrant from Palestine in 1921.*

Chapter Five

Between Wars

Jewish Immigration in the 1920s and 1930s

New Immigration Policies

After the end of World War I, thousands of Jewish immigrants prepared to leave war-torn Europe for the United States. However, many Americans were opposed to admitting a large number of new immigrants for fear that they would take jobs from Americans. Immigrants also were thought to pose a threat to American society. One U.S. official, exhibiting common prejudices, stated that many of these immigrants were "Polish Jews of the usual ghetto type. . . . They are filthy, un-American and often dangerous in their habits . . . mentally deficient, ill educated . . . [and] socially undesirable. . . . Ninety percent lack any conception of patriotic or national spirit."

Jews were also under suspicion in the United States because of their support of the Russian Revolution of 1917. Most Jews were pleased with the overthrow of Czar Nicholas II. They supported the new socialist government headed by Alexander Kerensky. In the United States, some Jews were members of the Socialist Party, while many others had joined labor unions. They believed that the unions and the principles of socialism, under which there was no private ownership and the government owned factories and farms, would help many poor working people achieve better lives. Socialism, they believed, would prevent the upper class from controlling all the nation's wealth, as it had in the past. But a year later, Kerensky's socialist government was overthrown by Communists. Led by Vladimir Lenin, the new Communist government gradually took control of Russia, renaming it the Union of Soviet Socialists Republics (USSR), or Soviet Union for short.

At first some Jews supported this Communist government, which took a more extreme view than socialism. Indeed, a few Jews even joined the American Communist Party. According to historian Howard Sachar, Jews made up almost half of the party's leaders. But most Americans feared that their country might be taken over by Communists and that their freedom would be lost. As a result, the so-called Red Scare swept across the United States. (The color red was closely associated with Communists.) Beginning in 1920, the U.S. government, led by Attorney General A. Mitchell Palmer, arrested suspected Communists and threw them into prison. On January 2, 1920, Palmer directed raids in 33 American cities. Police captured 4,000 suspected Communists, some of them Jews. Many of them were ordered to be deported, or sent away, from the United States. Palmer and other government officials believed that Jews were leading an effort by Communists to undermine the United States.

Jewish Immigration Facts

Because Jewish immigrants came from many countries, the number of Jews that entered the United States in any given year is often mixed in with immigration statistics for their countries of origin. Below are some highlights of Jewish immigration. These figures are all estimates.

Before 1850   There were about 15,000 Jews in America.

1840–1850   About 50,000 Jewish immigrants entered the United States.

1850–1860   Jewish immigration doubled from the previous decade to about 100,000.

1830–1900   About 300,000 Jews immigrated from Germany alone.

1900–1914   Approximately 1,447,000 Jews came to America from Russia.

1919   More than 119,000 Jews immigrated to the United States in one year.

1921–1924   About 153,000 Jews came to the United States before restrictive immigration laws were passed.

1948–2000   According to U.S. Citizenship and Immigration Services, 176,937 Jews have immigrated to the United States from Israel since the country's founding in 1948.

Through its actions the U.S. Congress seemed to agree. During the 1920s, Congress passed new laws reducing the number of immigrants that were allowed to enter America, especially those from eastern Europe. Jewish immigration fell from 120,000 in 1920 to 24,000 in 1922 and continued to decline over the next decade.

Jews also continued to face anti-Semitism in the United States. Some major universities restricted the number of Jews they would admit. Jews were also prevented from living in certain areas and from joining country clubs and other organizations. Leading law firms refused to hire Jewish attorneys. Some hospitals barred Jewish doctors from practicing in their facilities. Nevertheless, Jews continued to enter the legal and medical professions. Many of them, however, were not financially successful.

Among the leaders of American anti-Semitism was one of the world's most successful industrialists—Henry Ford. Beginning in 1908, the Model T Ford automobile had revolutionized transportation. Over the next two decades, Ford sold 15 million of these automobiles, becoming one of the wealthiest men in the United States.

In Michigan, where his cars were manufactured, Ford owned a newspaper called the *Dearborn Independent*. During the 1920s, the *Independent* published a series of anti-Semitic articles. These articles claimed that a vast conspiracy of Jewish bankers was planning to take control of the world. Some readers agreed with Ford's viewpoint. However, leading Jews as well as many other prominent Americans believed that Ford was totally mistaken in his beliefs. Many companies refused to do business with Ford. The industrialist also faced an expensive lawsuit in court over the *Independent's* articles. In 1927, Ford finally apologized for the anti-Semitic statements published in his newspaper. He sold the *Independent* not long afterward and was quoted as saying, "No one can charge that I am an enemy of the Jewish people. I employ thousands of them."

Jewish Success Stories

Despite the anti-Semitism that they faced, many Jewish immigrants managed to achieve great success. One of them was Helena Rubenstein. Born in Poland in 1902, Rubenstein traveled to Australia, where some of her family was already living. There she opened a small business that produced women's face cream. The ingredients for the face cream had been developed by Rubenstein's mother. Rubenstein eventually opened beauty shops in Australia, Europe, and New York City, where she made her home. Helena Rubenstein's cosmetics became one of the world's most famous brands. Rubenstein was recognized as one of America's most successful business leaders in the mid-20th century.

Jewish businesswoman Helena Rubenstein, photographed in 1934, was born in Poland and eventually made her home in the United States.

Jewish Americans also continued to achieve success in the entertainment business. Samuel, Jacob, and Levi Shubert, for example, the sons of poor Russian Jewish immigrants, began their careers working at a theater in Syracuse, New York. In 1900, they bought their own theater in

New York City. Five years later, they owned 13 theaters and, by 1914, the Shubert brothers were running theaters across America. The Shuberts also produced their own plays and hired famous actors to appear in them. By 1929, an estimated 75 percent of all the plays in New York City were being produced by the Shuberts.

Jews also entered the motion picture business. During the early part of the 20th century, silent pictures—in which the voices of the actors were not heard—were being shown in vaudeville theaters in many towns and cities. The pictures were played on machines called nickelodeons, into which a customer inserted a nickel. Adolph Zukor, a poor Hungarian Jewish immigrant, recognized the opportunities available in the nickelodeon business. Zukor and a friend, Marcus Loew, pooled their money and opened a nickelodeon on Broadway in New York City. Gradually they expanded their business, opening nickelodeons in other cities along the East Coast. With the money from this venture, Zukor began producing feature films. Eventually, Zukor realized that he needed a chain of movie houses to show his films. By the 1920s, Zukor was running Paramount Pictures, the largest film distributor in the United States. Today, Paramount is still a major film production company.

Soon after this photograph was taken in 1920, Louis B. Mayer helped start a film production company called Metro-Goldwyn-Mayer (MGM).

Another successful Jewish movie producer was Louis B. Mayer. Mayer's family came from Minsk, Russia, and settled in Canada. In 1904, at age 19, Mayer left Canada and moved to Boston. There he purchased a 600-seat theater, the Gem, just outside the city. The theater attracted large audiences. With the money he made, Mayer started his own film company. By 1918, Mayer was making films in Los Angeles, California, which was already the center of the motion picture business. Six years later, he was running Metro-Goldwyn-Mayer (MGM). MGM became one of the most successful production companies in the film business.

Jewish Composers

When plays and silent films were produced, they were accompanied by music. Many musical compositions were created in an area of New York City known as Tin Pan Alley. The name originated because musicians were pounding out new songs on pianos that sounded to some like the banging of tin pans. Among the musicians playing in Tin Pan Alley were George and Ira Gershwin. Their parents, Rosa and Moishe Gershovitz, were Jewish immigrants who had come to Brooklyn, New York, from St. Petersburg, Russia. George and Ira composed the hit song "Swanee" in 1919. It sold over a million copies. In 1924, George Gershwin composed perhaps his best-known piece of music, "Rhapsody in Blue." It combined the sounds of jazz and classical music. The Gershwins also wrote musical shows for Broadway and the movies.

Another famous composer from Tin Pan Alley was Irving Berlin. A Russian Jewish immigrant who came to America in 1893, Berlin first worked in New York as a singing waiter. Gradually he began composing songs. Among his best-known works are "White Christmas" and "God Bless America." Berlin also wrote a string of successful musicals on Broadway during the 1930s. As one expert said, "Irving Berlin has no *place* in American music. He *is* American music."

The Great Depression

By the 1930s, the United States was stuck in a worldwide economic crisis known as the Great Depression. Jobs were scarce during the Great Depression. Approximately 25 percent of the population was unemployed, among them many Jewish immigrants. As a result, Jewish immigrants often faced severe anti-Semitism. Many non-Jews did not want to compete with Jews or any other immigrants for the few jobs that were available.

In politics, however, Jews discovered new opportunities. Along with other immigrant groups, such as the Irish, many Jews joined the Democratic Party. In 1933, Americans elected a Democratic president, Franklin D. Roosevelt. The new president promised that his administration would deal with the problems caused by the Great Depression. Roosevelt called on many people, including Jewish immigrants, to help him. As historian Howard Sachar wrote, "Roosevelt opened wide the doors of his government to talented Jews." Among Roosevelt's advisers was a prominent Jewish lawyer and immigrant named Felix Frankfurter. Roosevelt would later nominate Frankfurter to the U.S. Supreme Court. Another Jew, Henry Morgenthau Jr., served as Roosevelt's secretary of the treasury.

This did not mean, however, that anti-Semitism had suddenly disappeared in the United States. Hitler had come to power in Germany in 1933. Soon afterward, the Nazis instituted laws that discriminated harshly against Jews. The Nazis would soon write a dark chapter in Jewish history. It would have a terrible impact on America's Jewish immigrants. ❖

Opposite: When U.S. troops liberated the Nazi-run Buchenwald concentration camp in Germany in April 1945, they found and photographed inmates such as these Jewish men, who were weak, starving, and lucky to be alive.

Chapter Six

The Holocaust
and Its Aftermath

World War II

Nazi Germany

Adolf Hitler made no secret of his attitude toward Jews. In his speeches and writings, he blamed them for the German defeat in World War I. He also vowed that their influence in Germany would be eliminated if he came to power. In 1933, when he became chancellor of Germany, Hitler immediately began to put his anti-Semitic policies into effect. The Nazis opened a concentration camp at Dachau, Germany, where Jews and other so-called Nazi enemies were to be imprisoned. Jews were among Dachau's first prisoners, and they were beaten and later murdered by Nazi guards.

About 37,000 Jews were fortunate enough to leave Germany during this time to immigrate elsewhere. Among them was the world-famous scientist Albert Einstein, who was offered a position at Princeton University in New Jersey. Nevertheless, highly restrictive immigration laws prevented many other Jews from entering the United States. Only 4,000 to 5,000 German Jews were able to enter the United States in 1934 and 1935.

Meanwhile, inside Germany the plight of the Jews grew steadily worse. At a spectacular rally of thousands of Nazi supporters in 1935, Hitler decreed the Nuremberg laws. Under these laws, Jews were stripped of their German citizenship. Jewish lawyers and doctors were no longer permitted to practice, and Jewish merchants were forced to sell their businesses to Gentiles. While many Jews were now convinced that immigrating to the United States was their best hope to have a decent life, and possibly to survive at all, the restrictive U.S. immigration laws remained in effect. Furthermore, so they would not become a burden on the U.S. economy during the Great Depression, immigrants had to prove that they had enough money to support themselves or that they had families to support them. This was extremely difficult for most, however, because the Nazis forced emigrating Jews to leave most of their money behind.

Meanwhile, the Nazis opened new concentration camps in Germany at Buchenwald and Sachsenhausen. In 1938, Hitler took control of Germany's neighbor, Austria. Austrian Jews were now driven from their homes and businesses. Others were taken to another new concentration camp at Mauthausen, Germany. On November 9 and 10, 1938, Hitler unleashed his Nazi troops against the Jews throughout Austria and Germany. The Nazis destroyed Jewish synagogues, shops, and homes, murdered some Jews, and brutally beat others. The incident was known as Kristallnacht—the Night of Broken Glass—because the glass windows of many Jewish homes and businesses were shattered by Nazi thugs.

The *St. Louis* Affair

Jews who could afford to leave Germany in the 1930s tried desperately to find other places to live. In May 1939, hundreds of Jews bordered the ship *St. Louis* in Hamburg, Germany. They were bound for Havana, Cuba, where the government had offered to admit them. There they planned to wait until they could legally emigrate to the United States. By the time the *St. Louis* arrived in Havana, however, the Cuban government had changed its immigration laws and refused to admit the Jews. The American Jewish Joint Distribution Committee (the "Joint") offered to pay the Cuban government to admit the Jews, but Cuban authorities would not accept the money. The *St. Louis* left Havana and headed for Florida. But officials there, following U.S. immigration laws, also refused to let them enter the country. Some of the Jews aboard the ship tried to contact President Roosevelt, but the president did not respond. As a result, the *St. Louis* was forced to return to Germany with its hundreds of Jewish immigrants. According to historian Arthur Hertzburg, "most of its passengers ultimately perished in Nazi-held Europe."

Kristallnacht outraged many American Jews. It also spurred President Roosevelt to allow more Jewish immigrants to enter the United States. The Roosevelt administration eased immigration restrictions. From 1938 to 1941, more than 100,000 Jewish immigrants left Europe and came to the United States. However, Roosevelt still had to act carefully. In 1939, more than 80 percent of Americans said they were opposed to admitting more immigrants into the country.

Jewish residents of Warsaw, Poland, surrendered to Nazis in 1943 after the Nazis put down an uprising of the city's Jews against their persecutors.

The Holocaust

On September 1, 1939, Nazi troops invaded Poland, beginning World War II. Poland fell to the Nazi forces in less than a month. Hitler ordered that Polish Jews should be either shot or rounded up and moved into ghettos. Jews were forced to leave their country villages and move into Polish cities such as Warsaw, Lublin, and Lodz. There many of them died from lack of food or housing. Others were taken to yet another concentration camp, called Auschwitz, which was opened in 1940. That year, Nazi troops stormed across western Europe, conquering almost all the nations in the area. Now western European Jews found themselves at the mercy of the Nazis.

Some Jews were fortunate enough to escape. Composer Darius Milhaud, who lived in Paris, later wrote, "I realized clearly that the [occupation] would prepare the soil for . . . monstrous persecutions." With his wife Madeleine and their children, Milhaud left Paris in their car. The family headed west toward the French border with Spain. "We set out in an exceptionally violent thunderstorm," Milhaud wrote. "We were stopped several times along the way for our [immigration] papers to be examined. The roadblocks grew more and more numerous. . . . We had to explain our position and show our passports and our tickets for the [ship]." Eventually they reached Portugal, which was not under Nazi control. At the port city of Lisbon, the family boarded a ship for the United States.

Once any such Jewish refugees reached the United States, they often encountered new problems. There were few jobs, and those that were available paid little money. Gertrude Hirschler fled Europe for Baltimore, Maryland. As she recalled, a family of four could manage to live on $25 per week. However, many refugee families could earn only $15 weekly.

Even so, conditions in the United States were far better for Jews than in Nazi-occupied Europe. Early in 1942, Nazi officials met at Wannsee, a suburb of Berlin, Germany. There, at Hitler's orders, they discussed the Final Solution—the total extermination of Europe's Jews. The Nazis had decided on a policy of genocide.

This term refers to the complete destruction of a race of people. This genocide is known today as the Holocaust.

More new concentration camps were erected in Poland at Sobibor and Treblinka. At the camps, instead of shooting Jews, the camp guards now used poisonous gas to execute them by the thousands. Carbon monoxide was used at some of the camps. At Auschwitz, guards began using a gas called Zyklon B. This gas was originally designed as a pesticide to kill insects.

Surviving child prisoners were photographed at the Auschwitz concentration camp in Poland when the camp was liberated by Soviet troops in January 1945.

Israel Green, a Jewish diamond cutter from Belgium, was taken to Auschwitz in 1942. "They put us on a train," he said. "We couldn't stand, we couldn't sit. It was like sardines. It took three days. . . . No water. No food. Did people die? Oh, and how!" Eventually, this train, like hundreds of others, arrived at Auschwitz. There the passengers were separated. The elderly, the weak, and many of the children were ordered to one side. They were later told by the Nazi camp guards to take off their clothes so they could bathe in the showers. Instead, they were taken to a gas chamber and killed with Zyklon B.

Green was more fortunate. "They took me to work. I [carried] cement on my back. . . . One hundred fifty pounds. And breaking rocks with picks, with shovels." The inmates were given very little food. Green, however, who had many gold fillings in his teeth, found a way to get more food. He removed the fillings and gave them to the guards in return for food. Some inmates tried to escape, but they were caught. The guards "took off [the inmates'] clothes from them and everybody must see this," Green recalled. "Then they hang them . . . [and] leave the people twenty-four hours." Green was among the few who survived the horrors of Auschwitz. Approximately 4 million people, mostly Jews, were killed there.

Reports Reach the West

In December 1941, the United States entered World War II when President Roosevelt declared war on Japan after the Japanese attack on the U.S. naval base at Pearl Harbor, Hawaii. The United States also went to war against Nazi Germany, which was allied with Japan.

By the middle of 1942, reports were already coming out of Poland about the mass executions of Jews by the Nazis. At first, these reports seemed unbelievable. But by the end of the year, the Holocaust had been confirmed as fact. Late in 1942, Rabbi Stephen Wise, a Jewish leader in the United States, discussed the Holocaust with the American press. President Roosevelt also made a statement expressing his horror over the Nazi genocide and warning the Nazis to stop.

Meanwhile, Jewish charitable organizations in the United States were working to enable some Jews to avoid the horrors of the Holocaust. These organizations included the Joint and the United Jewish Appeal (UJA), which had been founded in 1939. Money donated by American Jews through these organizations was used to feed about 600,000 Jews in Poland. The money also allowed thousands of Jews to be transported out of Poland across Russia and eventually to China. Others were rescued from western Europe and taken to Portugal or Switzerland, both neutral countries.

In 1944, Henry Morgenthau convinced President Roosevelt to establish the War Refugee Board. This organization used money from the Joint to bribe Nazi officials, who released some Jewish prisoners from the concentration camps. According to one estimate, the board helped as many as 200,000 Jews escape the gas chambers.

Other than these efforts, little else was done by the United States to prevent millions of Jews from dying in the Holocaust. Some experts believe that President Roosevelt should have done more. But historian Arthur Hertzburg disagrees. He thinks that additional actions by the president would not have stopped the Nazis. As Hertzburg points out, the genocide was a central policy of Hitler's government. Even when the Nazis began losing the war by 1943, they increased their

It's a Fact!

About 500,000 Jews served in the American military during World War II. Almost 11,000 were killed.

efforts to murder Jews. Over the next two years, 850,000 Jews were exterminated at Auschwitz. In June 1944 alone, 400,000 Hungarian Jews were transported to Auschwitz to be killed.

Many Americans, however, did not believe that the Holocaust was real. They were more concerned about fighting World War II. Thousands of American soldiers were fighting in Europe and the Far East. The war itself, coupled with the high rate of anti-Semitism in the United States, left many Americans unwilling or unable to focus on the plight of Jews in Europe.

After the Holocaust

Only in 1945, when the war ended in Europe, did the full horror of the Holocaust become clear to the American people. As American soldiers entered the death camps, they saw what the Nazis had done there. One Jewish-American soldier, Howard Katzander, entered the Nazi death camp at Buchenwald. There he encountered 21,000 Jews so weak from hunger and disease that they could barely walk. He also saw the ovens where the Nazis had burned the bodies of Jews. "I saw bake ovens," Katzander recalled. "Instead of being used to bake bread they were used to destroy people. . . . There were various stories about how the victims were knocked out before they were 'baked,' and I saw one club which had been used for that purpose. There was also a table where gold fillings were removed from the teeth of skulls. There were long steel stretchers on which the prisoners, often still alive, were rolled into the stinking heat of the ovens."

After the war, Jews who had survived the concentration camps were taken to camps for displaced persons. Food was in short supply in these refugee camps. When President Roosevelt's successor, Harry Truman, heard about the conditions in the refugee camps, he immediately told the commanders of the U.S.

Army, "I know you will agree with me that we have a particular responsibility toward those victims of persecution and tyranny." With support from the government, conditions for the Jewish refugees began to improve. In addition, the Joint and the United Jewish Appeal used their funds to help the refugees. Under the direction of Dr. Joseph Schwartz, the Joint provided food for the refugees. In addition, schools were established for Jewish children, as well as hospitals for the sick.

A Jewish State

For decades, Jewish leaders around the world had been working to create a Jewish state, or nation, in the ancient holy land of Palestine. Their effort was known as Zionism (the word *Zion* is the traditional name for a Jewish homeland). As a result of the Holocaust, the Zionist movement took on new urgency. Many Jewish refugees wanted to leave Europe for settlements in Palestine. Many Arab settlers also lived in the area, however, so America's Jewish leaders lobbied President Truman to support the division of Palestine into two parts—a Jewish state, to be named Israel, and a part that would remain under Arab control.

President Truman eventually backed the establishment of Israel. A majority of American

Flying a homemade Israeli flag, Jews celebrate the official creation of a Jewish state in Palestine in 1948.

voters also supported a state for the Jews. Some Jews even left the United States to join the settlements in Palestine. Israel also received the endorsement of the United Nations, a world organization of 50 countries that was established in 1945.

Many officials in the U.S. government, however, opposed the creation of Israel. They feared that it would anger the Arabs. America was heavily dependent on Arab oil to power U.S. manufacturing plants and run American automobiles. Indeed, Arab nations in the Middle East violently opposed the establishment of a Jewish state. Nevertheless, in May 1948, the state of Israel was officially born. Arab forces immediately invaded Israel. But Israeli troops, which included some American Jews, drove the Arabs back and preserved the new nation.

Hadassah

Many Jewish Americans were strong supporters of Zionism. In 1912, Hadassah, a women's Zionist organization, was founded in the United States by Henrietta Szold. Szold led women to Palestine to provide medical care and education for Jewish settlers there. Today Hadassah is the largest women's organization in the United States.

A New Wave

Meanwhile, a new wave of Jewish immigrants began to enter the United States. Until 1948, the immigration laws had remained very restrictive. Only about 50,000 Jewish immigrants from war-torn Europe were allowed to come to the United States. However, in 1948 and again in 1950, new laws greatly increased the number of displaced persons who were permitted to immigrate. Between 1946 and 1952, more than 80,000 European Jews came to the United States.

Most of the new Jewish immigrants arrived in New York City. But others went to cities such as Baltimore, Boston, and Galveston, Texas. The new immigrants were assisted by volunteers from the Hebrew Immigrant Aid Society and the National Council of Jewish Women, who provided temporary housing, food, clothing, medical care, and instruction in English.

In the United States, the Jewish immigrants entered a world of expanding opportunity. More than 75 percent of Jewish Americans had advanced to jobs as company managers and other professionals. Jewish Americans were also among the highest salary earners in the United States.

For some of the new immigrants, however, the rise to the top would be very difficult. Among these refugees were many who had been imprisoned at the death camps. Most Americans, even fellow Jews, did not seem to fully understand their ordeal. At Auschwitz, for example, the inmates had been tattooed with identification numbers. Ruth Siegler recalled going to a dance where young Jewish American girls saw the number tattooed on her arm. "The girl next to me said: 'Oh, I didn't get a number.' Other people thought it was a telephone number." According to historian William Helmreich, American Jews were sympathetic to the survivors but could not offer much support. As Helmreich wrote, "The reluctance of the survivors to discuss what had happened, based in part on the lack of interest by American Jews, created a 'conspiracy of silence' that lasted for many years."

Indeed, many survivors did not want to describe the horrors that they had endured to those who had no way of understanding. The new refugees most often looked for support from members of their *landsmanschaften*, with whom they could discuss their common experiences in the Holocaust. Many of these immigrants spoke Yiddish rather than English and read Yiddish newspapers. Many married other Holocaust survivors. All of these things affected their ability to assimilate, that is, to become fully part of American society. As a result, Holocaust survivors formed a distinct group of immigrants.

The Rosenberg Case

As Jewish Holocaust survivors were trying to create new lives for themselves, they were shaken by a sensational espionage (spy) case involving Jews. Julius Rosenberg had been born in New York in 1918. An electrical engineer, Rosenberg joined an American Communist organization during the 1930s. Another member of the group was Ethel Greenglass. The couple fell in love and were married in 1939.

During World War II, Julius Rosenberg joined the U.S. Army Signal Corps, which was in charge of coordinating the U.S. Army's communications. But he also continued his work for the Communists, acting as a spy for the Soviet Union. He passed secrets about sophisticated American weapons to Soviet agents. Meanwhile, his wife's brother, David Greenglass, also a Communist, had gone to work for the U.S. government in Los Alamos, New Mexico, where scientists were developing an atomic bomb. Greenglass gave secret information on the development of the bomb to Rosenberg, who in turn transmitted it to Soviet agents.

In 1945, the United States was the only nation to possess the power of the atomic bomb. In 1949, however, the Soviet Union became the second country to develop this technology. U.S. government officials were stunned because they had not known that the Soviets had the ability to develop such a weapon.

Meanwhile, the Federal Bureau of Investigation (FBI) had been working undercover to expose the Soviet spy ring in the United States that included Julius Rosenberg and David Greenglass. Rosenberg and his wife, Ethel, along with Greenglass and other members of the spy ring, were arrested in 1950. Greenglass agreed to cooperate with the federal government and testify against the Rosenbergs. He was convicted of espionage and sent to prison for 15 years. The Rosenbergs, on the other hand, who were also found guilty of espionage, were sentenced to death. They were executed on June 19, 1953. Many years later, David Greenglass admitted that his sister, Ethel Rosenberg, had not been guilty of stealing atomic secrets after all. He had lied about her involvement to take the focus off himself and avoid harsh punishment for his role in the espionage.

By this time, the United States had entered into another period much like the Red Scare after World War I. Led by Senator Joseph McCarthy of Wisconsin, the U.S. Senate began investigations of people suspected of being Communists. At the same time, the House (of Representatives) Committee on Un-American Activities conducted similar investigations. Some of those accused were Jews, but many others were not. During the Rosenberg trial and the McCarthy era, Jewish immigrants faced a new wave of anti-Semitism. Many of the suspects' careers were ruined by these allegations. This period of "McCarthyism," as it was called, came to an end in 1954 when the U.S. Senate spoke out against Senator McCarthy and his unfair accusations of innocent people. ✡

Opposite: *A Jewish family lights a menorah, a special candleholder used during the annual eight-day celebration of Hanukkah.*

Chapter Seven

Migration and Immigration

1950s to Today

Most Jewish immigrants have settled
in these states.

To the Suburbs

I n the 1950s, many states and cities passed laws ending
discrimination in housing. This discrimination had prevented
Jews and other minorities from buying homes in many areas. Now
many Jews left cramped apartments in the cities and moved to the
outlying suburbs. In fact, in the years after World War II, a Jewish
real estate developer named William Levitt built a huge suburban
community called Levittown on Long Island, New York. This
suburb became home to more than 80,000 people. Levitt also
built similar communities in other parts of the United States.

Jews who moved to the suburbs brought their religion and
their culture with them. They established new synagogues. Many
of these were Reform and Conservative temples. Jews also started

religious schools, which educated Jewish children in the traditions of Judaism. In addition to the traditional bar mitzvah for boys, girls marked their coming of age in a similar ceremony called a bat mitzvah. The number of private schools for Jewish children, as an alternative to the public school system, increased too. From 69 Jewish elementary schools in 1946, the number grew to 463 in 1978.

Major Jewish Holidays

- **Rosh Hashanah,** the Jewish New Year, which occurs in September or October. (The traditional Jewish calendar differs from the modern-day calendar used in much of the world.)
- **Yom Kippur,** the Day of Atonement that ends the 10-day High Holy Day observance begun on Rosh Hashanah. On this day, Jews pray and fast (go without food) to atone (make up) for their sins.
- **Hanukkah,** an eight-day Festival of Lights celebrated in November or December of each year, the celebration of the rededication of the Jewish temple in Jerusalem and the oil that miraculously burned in the menorah (a special candle holder) for eight days.

- **Purim,** a celebration usually held in March marking the Jews' escape from a planned massacre because of the bravery of Queen Esther of Persia.
- **Passover,** a spring festival celebrating the Jews' escape from Egypt, held in March or April.
- **Shavuot,** which commemorates the giving of the Torah to the Jews on Mount Sinai, held in May or June each year.
- **Sukkot,** an autumn festival of thanksgiving celebrated in September or October. Sukkot celebrates the harvest and recalls the time the Israelites spent in the wilderness after they escaped from Egypt.

Like other people moving to the suburbs, Jews wanted to feel a sense of community. They no longer lived in the cities, surrounded by many other Jews. Synagogues and religious schools, in addition to serving as centers of Judaism, also offered Jews a chance to socialize with other Jews. To increase this sense of belonging, Jews also established community centers, which provided recreational activities for children and adults. The centers were often funded by local Jewish federations, which were charitable organizations that supported a wide variety of activities. All these Jewish organizations helped Jews deal with anti-Semitism they encountered. For example, once they reached the suburbs, Jews often found that they were barred from joining country clubs. A survey conducted by the Anti-Defamation League in 1961 revealed that two-thirds of the country clubs surveyed discriminated against Jews.

A Washington, D.C., grandfather teaches his grandchildren how to make challah, a traditional Jewish bread.

Jewish Cooking

Many Jewish dishes and foods have become popular in the United States. Among these is a sweet, braided bread called challah. It is often served at Shabbat, the Jewish Sabbath, and on Jewish holy days. Bagels spread with cream cheese and lox (smoked salmon) are eaten by Jews and many other Americans. According to one estimate, Jews have been eating bagels—chewy, doughnut-shaped rolls that are boiled and then baked—for 400 years. Jews also enjoy a traditional dish called matzo ball soup, a light chicken soup served with small dough balls made from eggs, seasoning, and crumbs of matzo, a flat bread. A popular Jewish snack is the knish, a pastry usually stuffed with mashed potato and onion or cheese. Blintzes, another popular dish, are thin pancakes rolled around cheese or fruit filling and baked or fried in a pan.

New Immigrants

As some Jews moved from America's cities to the suburbs, others came from Europe to the cities. Among them were Hasidic Jews. The Hasidim are an ultra-Orthodox group founded during the 18th century. Many Hasidic Jews were killed during the Holocaust. Those who remained found it difficult to reestablish a Hasidic community in Europe. As a result, they immigrated to Israel and the United States. Many of them established communities in Brooklyn, New York.

Other Jews came from the Soviet Union, which was formed after the czarist regime ended in Russia in 1917. Throughout history, Jews had faced persecution in Russia, which continued under the Soviet Communist government. To make matters worse, the Soviet Union had a strict policy against its citizens emigrating to other countries. During the 1960s and 1970s, however, more and more Soviet Jews began to demand that they be allowed to leave the country. The cry for freedom was taken up by prominent Jewish groups in the United States. They persuaded the U.S. government to put pressure on the Soviet leaders. Since the Soviets wanted to improve relations with the United States and open up greater trade, they agreed to permit more and more Jews to leave the Soviet Union. From 1970 to 1990, approximately 100,000 Jews left the Soviet Union for the United States. Many moved to large cities such as New York, Atlanta, and San Francisco.

Persecution acted as a force pushing Jews out of the Soviet Union. Jews in South America and Cuba also faced persecution from dictatorships. Some of these Jews escaped and came to the United States. Many settled in southern cities, such as Miami, Florida. In addition, some Jews were pulled toward the United States by the promise of better education and jobs. Some of these Jews came from Israel. Between 1950 and 1990, about 500,000 Israeli Jews came to the United States.

Among them was young Itzhak Perlman. Born in Israel in 1945, Perlman developed the disease polio as a child. The illness permanently paralyzed Perlman so he could not walk. Nevertheless, his parents brought him to New York in the 1950s to study music at the famed Juilliard School. Perlman became an outstanding violinist who has played with every major orchestra in the world. He has also received four Grammy Awards, which are given to outstanding recording artists. Perlman plays classical, jazz, and klezmer music.

It's a Fact!

Klezmer music originated in eastern Europe during the Middle Ages (A.D. 350 to 1450). Combining folk and religious music, klezmer bands use a variety of instruments including trumpets, clarinets, violins, and drums. Klezmer music is often played at Jewish celebrations, such as weddings.

Politics, Culture, and the Professions

During the last part of the 20th century, Jews achieved a strong presence in American politics. They voted overwhelmingly for John F. Kennedy, who became president of the United States in 1960. Among Kennedy's closest advisers was a Jewish historian named Arthur M. Schlesinger Jr. Kennedy also appointed Connecticut governor Abraham Ribicoff and attorney Arthur Goldberg, both Jews, to his cabinet. After Kennedy was assassinated in 1963, he was succeeded by Vice President Lyndon Johnson. President Johnson appointed Goldberg to the U.S. Supreme Court.

It's a Fact!

Jonas Salk was born in 1914 to Jewish immigrant parents from Russia. Salk graduated from New York University Medical School and became a research scientist. In 1952, he developed a vaccine to prevent the devastating disease polio. This vaccine saved countless children from paralysis or even death.

In 1967, war broke out in the Middle East between Israel and several Arab states. Israel had wide support in this war, known as the Six-Day War, from the United States. In fact, about 10,000 young Jewish Americans volunteered to go to Israel and serve in the Israeli army during the war. The war ended when Israel defeated its Arab enemies, greatly enlarging the size of the Jewish state. In 1973, on Yom Kippur, a Jewish holy day, war broke out again in the Middle East. Once again, Israel received strong support from the United States that helped the Jews defend their territory. Among the leaders involved in creating a peace settlement between Jews and Arabs after the Yom Kippur War was U.S. Secretary of State Henry Kissinger, a Jew.

In addition to prominent positions in politics, Jews also achieved recognition in literature. Saul Bellow, a Canadian Jew, immigrated to Chicago, where he spent much of his early life. In 1944, Bellow published his first novel, *Dangling Man,* followed by other works over the next three decades. His novel *Humboldt's Gift,* published in 1975, won the Pulitzer Prize in literature. A year later, Bellow was awarded the Nobel Prize in Literature, the world's most prestigious literary award.

Another Nobel Prize winner was Isaac Bashevis Singer. Born near Warsaw, Poland, in 1904, Singer was the son of a rabbi. He worked as a journalist, then immigrated to the United States in 1935. In his book *In My Father's Court,* published in 1966, Singer described the Yiddish culture of the Jews of Eastern Europe. Singer published other books in the 1970s, eventually receiving the Nobel Prize in 1978.

Another Jewish writer, Elie Wiesel, was born in 1928 in the eastern European country of Romania. In 1944, Wiesel and the rest of his family were taken by the Nazis to the death camp at Auschwitz. Wiesel and his two older sisters survived. After the war, he published the book *Night* about the experience of the death camps, and he became a U.S. citizen in 1963. In addition to teaching and writing, Wiesel has also become an influential speaker on the

Nobel Peace Prize–winner and Holocaust survivor Elie Wiesel was photographed in 2004.

Holocaust. In 1978, Wiesel was named chair of the United States Holocaust Memorial Council, which has worked to memorialize the Holocaust in the United States by establishing museums and educating Americans about the tragedy. In 1993, under the direction of the United States Holocaust Memorial Council, the U.S. Holocaust Museum opened in Washington, D.C. In addition, American schools have started to include educational programs describing the Holocaust and its impact on Jews in Europe and the United States.

The 21st Century

Jewish immigration continued during the last two decades of the 20th century and into the 21st century. Between 1980 and 2003, approximately 400,000 Jewish immigrants were assisted by the Hebrew Immigration Aid Society. These immigrants found that most doors were open to them in education and in careers. Indeed, many Jewish immigrants came to the United States to seek educational opportunities. Some received scholarships from organizations such as the Israel Sephardic Education Fund (ISEF).

Among these students was Miriam Bitton. Bitton's parents were Jews who had moved to Israel from the North African nation of Morocco. Her father, who worked for the Israeli government, would sometimes take her with him to watch trials in the local court. Bitton was very interested in how the courts worked, and she hoped to become a judge. Although her parents were poor, they made sure that Bitton and her four siblings got a good education and gave them, in her words, "a deep sense of morality and idealism, but they were unable to give us much on a material level." With a scholarship, however, Bitton emigrated to the United States, where she attended the University of Michigan Law School. Over four years she was given $32,000 by the ISEF.

Another student immigrant to the United States from Israel is Aviva Zeltzer-Zubida. With the help of a scholarship, she and her husband and their baby could afford to come to the United

States. The couple lives in Brooklyn, New York, in a community of Jewish immigrants. "ISEF allowed me to continue studying," Zeltzer-Zubida said, "but it's more than that. It's about finding a community of people who care, who share your goals and world view." Tomer Levi is a Jewish immigrant who is studying at Brandeis University in Massachusetts. His ancestors came from Lebanon and Iraq. He emphasized that help from ISEF allowed him to "stay focused on my academic duties without having to worry about rent payments."

Jewish immigrants have also continued to come from the former Soviet Union, especially from Bukhara, a city in Uzbekistan, located in west Asia. Starting in the last decades of the 20th century, between 50,000 and 60,000 Jewish immigrants from Bukhara have come to live in the New York City area.

Other Jews have immigrated to the Midwest. Among them is Anastasia Murzin, a Russian Jewish student who lives in Fort Wayne, Indiana. Through a Jewish student organization there, she has met other Jewish students from cities such as Chicago, Illinois, and Milwaukee, Wisconsin. They gather for special Shabbat services and attend programs to talk about Judaism. Several thousand other Jewish students have immigrated to the United States from Europe, Ethiopia (an African nation), and Latin America.

These students did not have to face the anti-Semitism that had confronted immigrants in the past. Nevertheless, some problems remained. During the early 1980s, for example, attacks on Jewish synagogues occurred. Some synagogues were burned.

Others were painted with Nazi symbols. Although these incidents declined over the next two decades, they did not disappear. In 1999 and 2000, the Anti-Defamation League reported more than 3,000 anti-Semitic incidents. These included attacks on Jews and Jewish synagogues.

Nevertheless, Jews continued to advance in American society. In 2000, a Jewish senator from Connecticut, Joseph Lieberman, was selected to run for vice president by Democratic presidential candidate Al Gore. Lieberman was the first Jew to be chosen for this position. Although the Democrats lost the election, Lieberman returned to the Senate and ran for the Democratic presidential nomination himself in 2004. Even though he did not get the nomination and therefore would not run for president, the fact that Lieberman and other Jews were welcomed at this level of the American political establishment shows just how much Jews have achieved in the United States.

Senator Lieberman is a practicing Jew who attends services regularly. However, today's Jewish leaders are concerned that others are drifting away from their Jewish faith. They point to the rise in intermarriages between Jews and Gentiles. These intermarriages had risen to more than 50 percent among Jews, which means that more than half of Jewish Americans marry non-Jews. While some of these families raise their children in the Jewish faith, many do not. Meanwhile, the number of Jews has been declining because Jewish families are having fewer children. And while Jewish immigration continues today, the number of immigrants is not great enough to make much of a difference in the Jewish population of the United States.

These developments were occurring just as more and more Jews were achieving power and prosperity in American society. And while this situation creates new challenges for the 21st century, Jewish Americans can be proud of a truly impressive legacy of success in the United States.

Time Line of
Jewish Immigration

1654	First Jewish immigrants arrive at New Amsterdam.
1700–1770	Jews establish congregations in New York City; Newport, Rhode Island; Philadelphia, Pennsylvania; Charles Town, South Carolina; and Savannah, Georgia.
1775–1781	Jewish immigrants fight for the Patriot cause against the British.
1789	The Bill of Rights assures religious freedom for all Americans, including Jewish immigrants.
1830s	A wave of German Jewish immigrants comes to America.
1843	B'nai B'rith, the first Jewish fraternal organization in the world, is founded in New York City.
1847	More than 50,000 Jewish immigrants and their descendants live in the United States.

1861–1865	More than 6,000 Jewish soldiers and sailors fight for the North and over 3,000 fight for the South during the Civil War.
1870s	Jewish immigrants start arriving in large numbers from eastern Europe.
1883	Emma Lazarus writes the poem "The New Colossus."
1909	Clara Lemlich leads a strike against garment manufacturers in New York City.

1911	The Triangle Factory fire results in labor reforms spurred by Jewish immigrant groups in New York.
1913	Leo Frank trial and murder demonstrate anti-Jewish sentiment in United States.
1913	Anti-Defamation League of B'nai B'rith founded.

1916	Louis D. Brandeis becomes the first Jew nominated to the Supreme Court.
1917–1918	More than 250,000 Jewish Americans join the U.S. Army and U.S. Navy during World War I.
1920s	Restrictive U.S. laws reduce Jewish immigration.
1930s	Thousands of Jewish Americans become unemployed along with other Americans during the Great Depression. Anti-Jewish sentiments rise among many Americans.
1933	President Franklin Roosevelt appoints two prominent Jewish men to his cabinet to help the nation overcome the depression.
1938–1941	More than 100,000 Jews immigrate to the United States to escape the Nazi takeover of Europe.
1941–1945	Millions of European Jews are killed by Nazis during the Holocaust.
1948	Jewish state of Israel is established. U.S. immigration laws are changed to admit more Jews.
1950s	New, less restrictive immigration laws allow more Jewish immigrants to enter the United States, especially from Europe.
1953	Julius and Ethel Rosenberg are executed for spying.
1960	Two Jews are named to President John F. Kennedy's cabinet.
1967	Israel wins the Six-Day War.
1973	Yom Kippur War breaks out between Israel and Arab states.
1970–1990	100,000 Soviet Jews come to United States.
2000	Connecticut senator Joseph Lieberman becomes the first Jew to be nominated for vice president of the United States.

Glossary

anti-Semitism Hatred of and prejudice against Jews.

assimilate To absorb or blend into the way of life of a society.

congregation Religious community.

culture The language, arts, traditions, and beliefs of a society.

emigrate To leave one's homeland to live in another country.

ethnic Having certain racial, national, tribal, religious, or cultural origins.

Gentile A non-Jew.

Holocaust Mass killings of the Jews in Europe by Nazis during World War II.

immigrate To come to a foreign country to live.

kosher Permitted to be eaten by Jews according to their dietary laws.

prejudice Negative opinion formed without just cause.

rabbi Jewish religious teacher or leader.

refugee Someone who flees a place for safety reasons, especially to another country.

Shabbat Jewish Sabbath or day of worship.

stereotype Simplified and sometimes insulting opinion or image of a person or group.

strike Workers' refusal to work until they receive higher pay or other benefits.

synagogue Jewish house of worship.

Zionism Efforts by Jews to establish a national homeland.

Further Reading

BOOKS

Altman, Linda Jacobs. *The Impact of the Holocaust.* Springfield, N.J.:
Enslow Publishers, 2004.

Berger, Gilda. *Celebrate! Stories of the Jewish Holidays.* New York:
Scholastic, 2002.

Buxbaum, Shelley M. *The Jewish Faith in America.* New York:
Facts On File, 2003.

Diner, Hasia. *A New Promised Land: A History of Jews in America.*
New York: Oxford University Press, 2003.

Frank, Anne. *The Diary of a Young Girl.* New York: Bantam Books, 1993.

Rubin, Susan Goldman. *L'Chaim! To Jewish Life in America! Celebrating from
1654 until Today.* New York: Abrams, 2004.

WEB SITES

The History Place. "Holocaust Timeline." URL: http://www.history-
place.com/worldwar2/holocaust/timeline.html. Downloaded on
August 18, 2004.

Jewish Holidays and Festivals on the Net. URL:
http://www.melizo.com/festivals. Downloaded on August 18, 2004.

Judaism 101. URL: http://www.jewfaq.org. Downloaded on
August 18, 2004.

United States Holocaust Memorial Museum.
URL: http://www.ushmm.org. Downloaded on August 18, 2004.

Index